Literacy Smarts

Simple classroom strategies for
using interactive whiteboards
to engage students

JENNIFER HARPER

BRENDA STEIN DZALDOV

Foreword:

DAVID BOOTH

Pembroke Publishers Limited

Dedication

For Jenny, Mitch, Benji and, of course, Ophir. I love you. — BSD

To Casey, for making everything possible, and to Dean and Jack who wrote books with Mommy. — JAH

© 2011 Pembroke Publishers
538 Hood Road
Markham, Ontario, Canada L3R 3K9
www.pembrokepublishers.com

Distributed in the U.S. by Stenhouse Publishers
480 Congress Street
Portland, ME 04101
www.stenhouse.com

We acknowledge the financial support of the Government of Canada through the Book Publishing Industry Development Program (BPIDP) for our publishing activities.

We acknowledge the assistance of the Government of Ontario through the Ontario Media Development Corporation's Ontario Book Initiative.

Library and Archives Canada Cataloguing in Publication

Harper, Jennifer
   Literacy smarts : simple classroom strategies for using interactive whiteboards to engage students / Jennifer Harper & Brenda Stein Dzaldov.

Includes bibliographical references and index.
Issued also in electronic format.
ISBN 978-1-55138-267-8

   1. Interactive whiteboards. 2. Teaching—Aids and devices. 3. Educational technology. 4. Education, Elementary—Audio-visual aids. I. Stein Dzaldov, Brenda II. Title.

LB1043.5.H37 2011   372.133'5   C2011-904789-6

eBook format ISBN 978-1-55138-829-8

Editor: Kat Mototsune
Cover Design: John Zehethofer
Typesetting: JayTee Graphics Ltd.

Printed and bound in Canada
9 8 7 6 5 4 3 2 1

MIX
Paper from
responsible sources
FSC® C004071

Contents

Foreword

Welcome to the digital world of today's classrooms. Now we can bring the outside world into our school spaces, and we can remove our walls and take the school outside into the global sphere, all with Web 2.0 tools. Sounds wonderfully simple, until you confront those 25 students sitting in front of you inside a classroom with limited technological support, with new curriculum documents piled on your desk. And yet schools are indeed moving forward so quickly into the digital universe that we as teachers are sometimes overwhelmed, even flummoxed, by the complicated multimodal tools and resources that students are experiencing, usually outside school, but more and more frequently inside the classroom. We know that many of our students can connect us, wired and wireless, to different aspects of the technology, and work alongside us in discovering ways to promote learning and achieve the outcomes we are committed to. But there is much more for us to discover, and we are fortunate to have educators like Jennifer Harper and Brenda Stein Dzaldov to guide us in this discovery of how to incorporate tools of interactive teaching and learning into our quests for growth as contemporary and professional teachers.

The focus of this informative and supportive book is how the interactive whiteboard can be an entrance to the multimodal classroom as a learning commons, a place where students can act as agents of their own meaning-making, locating information and, more importantly, exploring and interpreting how to turn that data into knowledge. Jennifer and Brenda share with us the nuts and bolts of using interactive whiteboards, but they do much more: they open up possibilities for our students to become co-constructors of their own learning—now they have access to all the Web 2.0 tools every day, to maps, graphics, videos, research, texts, tables, charts. And it is not only access they have, but also control and management of all those modes as they interact with each other and with the data, expanding their critical and creative thinking.

I wish I had read this book last year when I was teaching my graduate course for teachers. I was working with them in a computer lab and I wanted to demonstrate a point. Turning around, I saw a white information board, picked up a marker, and tried to write on the board. When one marker didn't work, I tried another and another, until several teachers called out in shock, "David, that's an interactive whiteboard!" During the year, I took a workshop on how to make better use of this tool and now, having read this book, I am much more aware of the amazing support this invention has to offer in the classroom.

As a literacy educator, I want my repertoire of professional teaching/learning strategies to continue to evolve and, I hope, increase in scope. I may not be an inhabitant of the digital world, but I am certainly spending a great deal of my time there and enjoying it, and I want the students I work with to understand and make use of every single resource that can support them intellectually, emotionally, and socially. I need to incorporate technologies such as the interactive whiteboard into my classroom because they allow me to accomplish so much more than I could in the past. My students and I can be connected to a world community, and we can actually interact with each other in ways unknown to me even a few years ago.

This digital world causes me to teach literacy differently now; there is an endless number of text forms—in print, as image, with sound, and representing every subject imaginable; my students can engage with ideas, work with them collaboratively, record their efforts, classify and save them; they can develop their abilities as readers and writers while participating in authentic learning processes, expanding and enriching their literacy lives through technology and, especially, through the interactive whiteboard.

This book investigates the many ways that technology can extend our reach as teachers caring about developing students who will be prepared for a future where amazing new inventions will support their journey toward becoming thoughtful, skilled, and compassionate citizens. I am better prepared for these changes, strengthened by this informative and insightful book. I teach my literacy courses in a computer lab and I actually use the interactive whiteboard during each class. I must say that I now require technology in order to explore literacy education, and my students are better for it. Thanks, Jennifer and Brenda.

David Booth
University of Toronto

Introduction

The world of education is changing at a rapid pace, and much of that is due to advances in technology. New digital texts are always being created and our students are constantly interacting with them. There is no way for any teacher to know how to use every digital tool and keep current with every new text, application, or program. This book is not about staying current. Instead, it is about keeping an open mind to the amazing possibilities that technology—and specifically the interactive whiteboard—affords teachers and their students.

We know that our students are knowledgeable about and comfortable with technology. They are exposed to it every day. They play games on the computer. They receive and send e-mails. They text. They search for information on search engines and print out pictures and information when they are interested in a topic. They work, play, and socialize online. Even our youngest learners see their parents and family members on laptops, smartphones, and tablets. Digital technology is part of their home lives and, increasingly, part of their lives at school.

Interactive whiteboards, computers, and digital technology in our schools keep us in touch with the world of information that is an irrefutable part of our students' lives. The interactive whiteboard (IWB) creates virtually endless possibilities for teaching and learning. It provides access to graphics, photos, videos, moving images, and Web 2.0 tools. It allows the teacher to explain complex concepts to students by instantly accessing a world map, showing a video of a caterpillar morphing into a butterfly, or highlighting the patterns on a hundreds chart by a simple touch of the screen. It leads us into the future of learning—interpreting, managing, exploring, and expanding our students' thinking while enabling authentic learning.

This book not only builds on what we know about literacy development but also deals with the necessity that students think, interact, and engage with a wide variety of texts across all the content areas. Through the computer and the interactive whiteboard, the world is accessible from school. Not only are math, science, social studies, and the arts important content area subjects, but the literacy skills they require must be integrated when instructing the 21st-century learners in our classrooms. Literacy is embedded in almost everything we teach, whether it be planning a guided reading lesson focused on a particular reading strategy or framing questions on how students can apply their basic addition facts. As educators, we also know that literacy is a crucial part of how students learn. From reading a social studies text and having a student explain his/her thinking, to determining a solution in math and explaining it to a small group, to writing a nonfiction report, the basics of literacy are an essential part of student learning. The foundation of literacy development will always be based on the ability to use the skills of reading, writing, speaking, listening, and viewing. With the interactive whiteboard, we can build a solid foundation in literacy skills and incorporate the texts, content, and pedagogy that engage and educate our students.

Although the interactive whiteboard has often been used as a glorified whiteboard or a screen to show movies or slide presentations, it has the potential to be much more than that. In addition to being a tool to access the wide variety of textual resources available, the interactive whiteboard can be used in assessment *for*, *as*, and *of* learning. It can be used to easily place, organize, sort, and expand on ideas. Steps in a process as well as final products can be saved, revisited, and ultimately evaluated using the interactive whiteboard and other digital tools. The interactive whiteboard is capable of giving specific, timely, and accurate feedback to learners as they interact with content and practice skills. It is a safe space for students to learn, make mistakes, and expand their learning. It is a place for collaborative learning communities to work, provides opportunities for oral language practice, and offers a space to scaffold all areas of content and literacy instruction. The interactive whiteboard opens a window to the world by linking the classroom community to the Internet and all the information, creativity, and innovation that interaction allows. Our objective is to share ways to use technology—specifically incorporating the interactive whiteboard—to attempt creative, engaging activities that deepen students' learning and critical thought, but also incorporate the important elements of effective teaching that all teachers know about, think about, and plan for.

The 21st-Century Learner

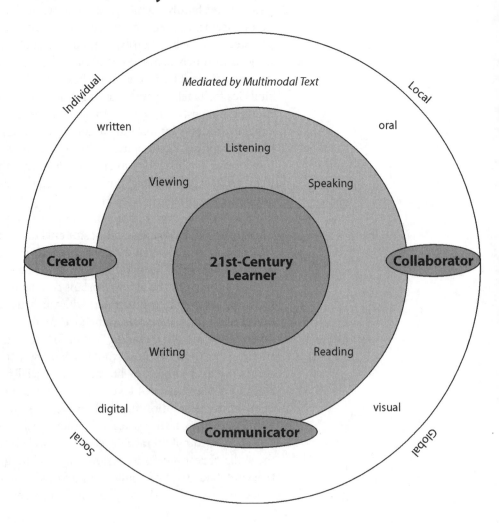

This graphic represents the 21st-century learner, and starts with the foundational literacy skills of reading, writing, listening, speaking, and viewing. These skills can be taught in a variety of creative ways; can be meaningful to learners; and can be applied to authentic reading, writing, and oral experiences, both at home and in the classroom. We no longer need to teach writing in a bound notebook with "red-blue-blue" lines, or define reading as the skill of "saying the words" in an English print text. The definitions of reading and writing have expanded to encompass a complex ability to decode, make meaning, and use text appropriately, in multiple languages and across many genres.

We conceptualize our students as creators, collaborators, and communicators who mediate their learning through interaction with multimodal text. With the 21st-century learner in mind, we will explore how the interactive whiteboard and other digital technology available in classrooms can serve as comprehensive tools for teaching and learning.

Literacy learning occurs in contexts that are individual: each experience has particular meaning for each individual, and that meaning depends on the individual's culture, history, background, identity, and language. But we know that literacy learning is also social: language and literacy truly have meaning only in a social context, as students interact with others. When a teacher reads aloud to a group of students, he or she must activate sufficient background knowledge to set the stage for each individual to understand a text, whether through listening or reading. That background knowledge might look different in each case, and the social setting (which includes the students in the class, the teacher, curricular demands, familial expectations, etc.) is an important component of how students understand and process language and information. The local community, practices, and purposes are an important part of the context for learning. Students and teachers are also influenced by the global community, to which we have immediate access through technology.

This book is organized in a way we hope will provide practical support for teachers. It interweaves educational theory, ideas, and strategies that offer suggestions for transfering traditional teaching into the digital world and that are supported by activities and lessons using the interactive whiteboard. You will find specific examples of Interactive Ideas; screenshots are included to illustrate some of the visual, graphic, and textual possiblities available to teachers using the IWB.

So join us on this ride along the path of 21st-century learning using digital technology and the interactive whiteboard. Remember that the ride might be bumpy at times; ultimately, you will reach a destination that will transform your teaching and your students' learning. As the great psychologist Jean Piaget said, "The principle goal of education is to create men and women who are capable of doing new things, not simply repeating what other generations have done."

1 Rethinking Literacy

Marc Prensky (2001) coined the term *digital native* to refer to today's student. Students are native speakers of technology, fluent in the digital language of computers, video games, and the Internet. He refers to those of us who were not born into the digital world as *digital immigrants*. We have adopted many aspects of the technology but, like those who learn another language later in life, we retain an "accent" because we still have one foot in the past. We will read a manual, for example, to understand a program before we think to let the program teach itself (Prensky, 2005).

An understanding of our students as digital natives is crucial to our instructional techniques and to using digital technology in the classroom to enhance instruction. Being digital natives, students might learn more effectively and be more engaged in the process if instruction is available in a digital format. As technology is constantly changing and developing, we can expand the possibilities for the digital natives in our classrooms. That said, teachers might be using the interactive whiteboard (IWB), but haven't considered all possiblities because they are still "reading the manual." Of course, it is the teacher's responsibility to make sure instruction is sound with respect to what we know about learning and literacy development. If we begin with what we know traditionally works, we can use that knowledge base to enter the digital world, creating many interactive and engaging possibilities for our students.

Understanding Our Students

Understanding students as literate individuals has always been a complex process. With the influx of technology, our role as teachers has changed. Years ago, "literacy" meant having a conversation, reading a book, or writing a story, note, or message. In the 21st century, literacy has shifted traditional classroom practice by reconceptualizing the learner and the text. We are still teaching the foundational skills involved in reading and writing—the alphabet and word families, sentence structure and spelling. However, the tools that we use to teach, be it an interactive whiteboard, tablet, or laptop, change the context for our students. Our students will be applying their knowledge of spelling patterns or global warming both locally and globally, and it is our job as their educators to provide them with the tools and skills to do this. A 21st-century approach looks at learners as individuals functioning in a social context, and we strive to make each learner literate by appealing to their strengths, motivations, and interests. It is a shift from a one-dimensional view of literacy learning to a new view that incorporates all the texts and tools that our students are confronted with daily.

Meaning is made in ways that are increasingly multimodal in nature. This means that we need to extend the range of literacy instruction so that it does not unduly privilege one type of text—print text—but instead brings into the classroom multimodal representations—such as graphic, oral, and digital—and particularly those integrated texts typical of the new media. The term "text" has changed to include digital technology, images, sounds, and even oral language (Booth, 2009).

Teaching Our Students

Literacy instruction and learning today involves all the literacies that students will engage in. It is how we define terms like *text* and *literacy* that will bring students into 21st-century learning. Understanding how to use and engage with text, including print, oral, and digital texts, is crucial in everything students do in school.

As our world changes with technology, our definition of text grows. It is much more than printed words in a book. For students, interacting with text involves everything from writing on a blog to manipulating information on a computer screen, or even interpreting a weather graph.

Here's an example of how a regular classroom routine might look different using an expanded definition of text and the interactive white board. The weather routine occurs most mornings in many primary classrooms. A student looks out the window to determine the weather and then chooses a pre-made card to place on a wall-mounted calendar to indicate that it is cloudy, sunny, rainy, or snowy outside. In rethinking this routine, we must ask ourselves what we want our students to understand when discussing the weather. Is it what the temperature means for them? Should they wear a coat or not? Is it cold enough that it might snow? Why is it usually colder in the morning? Can it be sunny in the morning and cloudy in the afternoon? Is the weather the same in Toronto and in Niagara Falls? Do graphs, maps, and charts help students understand the weather? We need to ask ourselves if we believe that collaborating, accessing information, understanding, and thinking about the weather is important for our students. This example illustrates how rethinking teaching enables us to open these possibilities for learning. By opening a link to a weather website each morning and revisiting it throughout the day, students can start to learn how temperature changes throughout the day and how the weather changes in different areas of the same city. By using a graphing program, students can track weather data, transform it into bar graphs, circle graphs, and charts. Students can watch videos about severe weather, or test their knowledge using simple games.

As teachers, we strive to connect to students' interests, experiences, and identities in order to make content more meaningful and relevant to them. Keeping digital natives in mind, there are many ways to engage students. Current theory tells us that students benefit from classrooms that encourage

- Student-centred learning: Teachers act as guides or coaches for students on the journey of learning.
- Student choice: Students are given a great deal of choice and freedom in paths to accessing information and ways to share their learning.
- Assessment *for* learning: Assessment is primarily focused around ongoing information that guides teaching and learning.
- Student diversity: Curriculum and instruction address student diversity and learning needs.
- Access: The classroom connects to a globalized, technological society.

Just as we broaden our understanding of literacy, we also need to adjust our definition of text.

A Grade 1 student reflected on the weather one fall day: "Ten degrees feels fresh." This quote was revisited in the spring, and the same student said, "Ten degrees feels warm." The instant access provided by the IWB allows students to click on previous ideas, think critically, and have a deeper understanding about what numbers mean and how they affect our daily lives.

- Integrated curriculum: Teaching core concepts and skills connecting two or more subject areas around a unifying theme or issue makes learning more engaging (Drake & Burns, 2004).
- Collaborative learning: Students work together with teachers, classmates, and others around the world.
- Higher-level thinking: Skills such as analysis, synthesis, and creating are goals of the learning.

The Foundational Skills

In the primary years, the foundational skills of literacy are important as students are introduced to the building blocks of literacy. As students enter the junior and intermediate years, they have a variety of literacy skills and strategies that provide a foundation for ongoing learning. As they apply these skills and strategies to more complex text and read for deeper meaning, they clarify and build upon the foundational literacy skills. For today's student, these foundational skills are embedded in the multiple literacies in the student's world.

Let us look closely at the basics in literacy: reading, writing, listening, speaking, and viewing. These are the five skills that we all use to help us gain from and share knowledge in the world around us. How can the interactive whiteboard assist with the teaching/learning of the foundational literacy skills?

Using the scaffolding approach to balanced literacy instruction, there are multiple ways to teach the foundational skills while engaging students at all points in their literacy development.

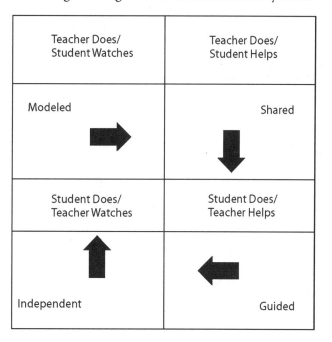

This chart shows the process of learning that involves scaffolding instruction and working with others. *Scaffolding* is used to describe the process of supporting students as they build new knowledge and skills. It involves
- breaking the knowledge and skills into small steps
- modeling the steps
- providing supports as students learn the steps
- gradually shifting the responsibility to students to apply the knowledge and skills independently

We know that collaboration with teachers and peers is crucial for learning. Gone are the days when people believed that students learned best sitting in neat rows, silently taking in the teacher's words. Instead, a culture of cooperation and collaboration is crucial as students and teachers talk, negotiate, and come to common understandings about knowledge and ideas. The skills of reading, writing, listening, speaking, and viewing must be taught in schools and we know these are vital. It is how we teach them that evolves. We can harness our students' experiences at home and the knowledge that they come to us with, and use that to create meaningful learning experiences in our classroom.

The interactive whiteboard can be a tool to teach and enhance the foundational skills. Students need to read, write, speak, listen, and view while deciphering a webpage or finding the important message in a podcast. And they are learning these basic skills while they are exploring and interacting with the wide range of texts in the digital world. Literacy is all around them, and it is up to us to help our students critically interact with the world they will one day be creating and expanding.

As David Booth once said, "The ball point pen was also rejected when it was first invented." But the accessibility of the pen enabled widespread literacy. Your use of the IWB as a tool will create ripples that will slowly change how you plan, instruct, and assess.

Listening, Speaking, and Viewing

The design of the interactive whiteboard strengthens listening, speaking, and viewing skills for both our students and ourselves. Rather than using an overhead projector to share information, with the speaker's back to the audience, using the interactive whiteboard places speakers face to face. Whoever is sharing information directly faces the listeners, and the audience can listen to and observe the speaker's body language, facial expressions, and voice. With the purchase and addition of a microphone, we can further enable students by adding another element to interactive activities.

Using the IWB microphone and speakers, a variety of options present themselves:
- Using the Record feature, you can create a song with the class and use a shape to point to each word as students sing the song. The song will be recorded, saving the movement and allowing you to play it again and have students view the shape the next time.

This screenshot shows a song copied from the Internet and pasted onto a SMART Board blank document. Students created a circle to follow along with the song. When the recording was played, the teacher moved the circle in time with the students' voices. When the song was replayed, the circle repeated the same movement to guide the students' repeated readings. Students then rewrote some of the lyrics by replacing specific words (e.g., *baa*, *sheep*) and by making up their own words, and the movement of the circle guided them in their rereading of the text.

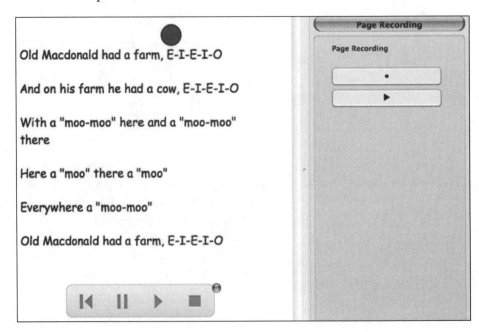

- Have students record their individual voices as they read a story to share later.
- Students can leave oral comments about a piece of work they wish to share with others; for example, for their parents during a parents' night.
- Students can leave a digital record of how they completed an activity, step by step.
- Students can create their own podcasts for events important to them. Both movement and voice are recorded, creating a file that can be replayed for a variety of reasons later.
- You can prepare students for independent work by recording a mini-lesson while demonstrating an activity on the screen. When you use "digital modeling," students can then re-view the lesson as they complete the task, and you can be engaged elsewhere.
- Students can record instructions for an activity they have completed for a group of students that follows.

Reading

Classrooms are rich in text. We stack our bookshelves and display colorful posters. We give students access to computers. We label items, bins, and workspaces. In junior classes, we teach students to write paragraphs and essays, fiction and nonfiction stories, reports and journals. In early primary classrooms, we write out songs, stories, facts, and poems. Placing an interactive whiteboard in the classroom extends the possibilities for reading outside the classroom walls.

Traditional

Students list the books they have read in logs, or complete worksheets describing the various aspects of the text. They might record comments in a reading response journal or create a file on the computer and record comments there, often in response to a prompt from the teacher. Sometimes, comments or book recommendations are posted in an area of the class for others to view.

IWB Advantage

When ideas are recorded on the interactive whiteboard, thoughts can be moved, added to, erased, or revisited. Pictures of a book cover can be imported as a visual representation of the book, and students can have comments interactively created on the IWB e-mailed to them at home if they are deciding which books to read. Students can share their thoughts by writing directly on the IWB below the picture of the cover. Students can use graphic images, such as stars, to rate books. You can compile a class Top 10 list, encouraging students to rate their favorite reads with the student response clickers. When you post a list of the class's top reads on the IWB, books become celebrated, discussed, and shared in an engaging and student-centred way.

An Interactive Idea for Independent Reading

Objective
To motivate preteens to read and critically analyze books read independently.

Hook
Post a picture of a book that has strong appeal in the classroom. Listen to the students' comments and write them around the book. Encourage students to record their own responses. Leave the slide up as an independent activity so students can access it throughout the day.

Lesson
1. Explain to students that they need to pick a book to read that they feel strongly about.
2. Have each student send in a picture of the cover of the book they choose and a justification as to why they selected the book.
3. Post one of the books and the student's justification on the IWB as students enter the class. During the attendance routine, have each student comment on the book: either that they did not read it, or their thoughts.
4. Circulate through a different book and interactive discusion each morning. This will expand your students' reading list, encouraging them to critically think about their reading and justify their thoughts.

Closure
Use this attendance routine as a prompt for discussion: *What other books sparked the same reaction? How would you alter the book? What does it remind you of? Can we classify the book into a genre?* Set up tables or charts and have the students move the book covers into various categories as they respond to the prompts.

Read-Alouds

Many authors have websites where they read their own books aloud on podcasts.

Think of that magical time where you share a special piece of children's literature with your students. A read-aloud can be an enchanting part of the day, when all is calm and everyone just listens to a story, when teachers model comprehension strategies and ask critical questions. While reading aloud, you can model a variety of skills: fluency, decoding, reading for meaning, thinking and predicting, etc. There are many interactive technologies available on the IWB to extend your classroom read-alouds.

Traditional

A teacher or other adult reads a story to students as they gather together at a whole-class meeting area. The teacher asks questions, models fluency, and prompts for comprehension. Student responses might be recorded on a chart paper or whiteboard, and posted as an anchor chart for future reference.

IWB Advantage

Using the IWB creates an interactive setting for a read-aloud. Stories can be read and reread by accessing an Internet link. Stories can be read by the author, the teacher, and others outside the classroom so students experience multiple interactive readings of the same text from a variety of perspectives. Students can listen to and view a variety of people reading stories. Family members can read a story to the class through an online phone call, regardless of where they are in the world.

An Interactive Idea for Critical Reading

Objective
To listen for fluency and intonation in read-alouds.

Hook
Read a children's book as a read-aloud. Choose a book with a pattern or rhythm that encourages fluency and expression; e.g., a book by Robert Munsch.

Lesson
1. Access a website where the author reads the book aloud in his own style. Select a book that was just read aloud in class by the teacher.
2. Create a two-column chart on a blank IWB page to compare how the teacher read the book to how the author read the book: *What are the important words/phrases? Why do you think Robert Munsch changed his voice, making it higher or lower?*
3. Replay the reading. The students listen critically to the text, deciding where to stress words or phrases. They listen for repetition and patterns to see how the author might emphasize certain elements of the book.
4. Post a copy of the text and have students use the pens to track the intonation of the speaker. Have the students change the intonation. *How does that change the text?*
5. Provide the students with one page of the book. Ask the students to practice reading it in groups or pairs. Ask them: *How will you read the text? What did you like that you heard already? What would you change in the reading of the page?* Students can record their own reading of the page in small groups, facilitated by the teacher.

Closure
For closure, introduce the terms *fluency* and *intonation*, describing it as "how an author reads smoothly and with meaning."

Extension
- To add another dimension to the classroom read-aloud, use an online phone system. Contact family members of students to read a story on the whiteboard or share their favorite memory. This adds another dimension to the task, as students are listening to and viewing a story being read. Ask students: *How did seeing a different reader read the story change the experience?*
- After the book has been read, ask students to think about a person they know who best represents the main character. Have them explain their choice. If possible, ask that person to read the voice of the main character so that students can discuss their decision after hearing the new version of the story. Ask them: *Did the voice you chose match the character? What did you like and what would you change?*

Ultimately reading aloud is one of the most engaging moments in a day, and one that students crave. The IWB does not lessen that magic, but can expand it beyond the walls of the classroom.

Shared Reading

Simply writing a short text—a sentence, poem, song, chant, story—on a piece of chart paper provides opportunities for students to practice shared reading, choral reading, repeated readings, predicting missing words, looking for rhymes, identifying high-frequency words, using word and letter patterns, and analyzing the structure of the text.

If you take this text and put it on the interactive whiteboard, you can still use all of these effective teaching strategies. You can also

- Have students clearly mark up the text you are teaching and easily erase mistakes, creating an errorless canvas.
- Keep the text on file. As you teach new skills, you can easily erase the old markings. As you change the learning focus, you can create new markings.
- Record the voices of your class reading the text and play it later, varying the volume of the reading to emphasize different parts, expressions, and words.
- Access a gallery or library and have students add meaningful visuals to the text that will differ according to students' interests and backgrounds.
- Add links to the text. For example, if the topic is the sun, you can create a link to a blazing animated sun, or to a site that gives information about the sun.
- After interacting with text with the whole class, erase the markings on the text and place it at a literacy centre with instructions for students to search for and mark up the text once again.
- Students can receive immediate feedback if you set the IWB to link to a reading of the text or parts of it. Students or the teacher can be recorded on a podcast and that link can be accessed for students to check their work through the link.
- To incorporate creative thinking, students can expand the text based on their understanding of language patterns and the message. Erase selected words and ask students to replace the spaces with new words that still make sense; have them justify their responses.
- Prompt students to change/rewrite stories using higher-order prompts, such as *summarize, compare, deconstruct, judge,* or *develop* a new story based on one of the elements of the story presented.

Independent Reading

One of the most treasured times for students is when they read independently in a quiet space, choosing their own books, browsing through them, absorbing the pictures, reading the words, and escaping into another world through text. Independent reading creates reading confidence, develops readers' skills, and builds a love of reading. By incorporating digital media, you can further extend the possibilities for independent reading in the classroom. There are various online tools that offer voice recording, allow feedback, and even provide assessment tools.

- Using a microphone, students can record their own voices.
- By listening to text recorded by themselves, peers, or teachers, they can hear fluent, expressive reading on self-selected stories.
- The recorded voice and text combination can also act as a running record, providing teachers with an assessment of student reading.

To follow up on students' reading:

- Create a blog where students can record the titles of books they have read. Provide prompts as the students respond to reading.
- Set up an online library, or create your own template on the IWB that contains all the titles of the classroom books. Students can search for titles and then click on a link that allows them to track and comment on the books they have read.

To extend these ideas further, websites offer primary teachers the opportunity to individualize a reading program for their students.

What is the best Halloween book you have read?

5 Approved Comments

Ethanucc

October 20, 2010 at 2:34 pm

Mummies in the Morning — Magic Tree House #3

Edit I Unapprove I Delete

Richarducc

October 20, 2010 at 5:14 pm

the dark hous!!!

Edit I Unapprove I Delete

Dimaucc

October 23, 2010 at 5:14 pm

My mom wrote a book about Halloween. It's cool!!!

Edit I Unapprove I Delete

Nigelucc

October 25, 2010 at 6:54 pm

Nate the great and the halloween hunt

Writing

An easy way to help promote correct pencil grip is to write on a vertical space. It is difficult for students to use a club grip when writing "on the wall."

The interactive whiteboard can also enable the technical skill of printing/writing. Students can use a finger or any object to write by applying pressure to the IWB. It will respond to any touch, creating a sense of empowerment for beginning writers and accessibility for those having difficulty with fine motor skills. The IWB can also support students struggling with pencil grip, as the vertical surface is a wonderful bridge to writing on a horizontal page.

At first, it does take some time to master holding the pens: for IWBs that work with a single touch, you cannot write if your hand drags on the screen. However, students will be so eager to print/write on the IWB they will figure out how to hold the pen properly, and that knowledge supports the transfer to gripping pencils or pens.

Modeled Writing

When you provide strong models of writing for your students, you help them understand your expectations. Use the blank template as your base to write a piece. Once a word is written on the IWB, it can be saved as a picture file. This allows you to touch and grab the words written, move them or delete them. Using the IWB, you can

- Outline an alphabet letter that young students are learning. Use the record feature and a graphic to model the movement of the pen for proper letter formation. Then have students follow the graphic with their pens to form their letters directly on the IWB. If you use a background of lined paper, students can practice writing with proper letter formation and spacing on an errorless canvas.
- Model editing skills, such as replacing words, correcting spelling, or changing the word order in sentences.
- Use the Recognize tool to identify the word that was handwritten. This offers instant feedback for students.
- Use different colors for writing or to highlight words to represent feedback from different sources (such as teacher or peer) or to focus on different concepts, such as expanding ideas or basic editing.
- Hide words with shapes, have students guess the word behind the shape, and then move the shape to check if they are right. This supports students in building vocabulary, predicting by using context clues, and collaborating to compose text.
- Erase all group editing marks and set up text as a centre for students to re-edit later.
- Post a piece of writing on a blog and invite comments from the local or global community.

These screenshots were created for a Grade 5 poetry lesson by teacher Kathryn O'Brien, connecting with a unit on energy usage. Each of the boxes is on a separate document. In this activity, the teacher modeled the format for the poem and left the instructions on the documents for reference. Students then worked in groups to create a poem. They could fluidly move between documents to review instructions, copy and paste created text, and drag it all together on the final screen. The IWB made it simple for groups to reference instructions and walk step-by-step through the process, while dragging and creating their own original work.

Write some "moems" (Poetry techniques) about your issue

-talk about the pros
-include the cons
-include your opinions about the other energy options

The sun's fingers creep to the solar panels

Shine, shine, shine on

Sun never runs out
It will stop the energy drought

Solar energy is like a fountain, it always flows

Finding your memorable ONE LINER

EVENT + YOUR FEELINGS
ex. use a song you love, and its
melody to inspire your new song!

Light up the city.
Our future is
bright!

Shine bright, Bryte City
Sun always shines
Sun, Sun, Sun

Your one liner can be repeated for power.

Organize your thoughts

One liner	One liner
"MOEM"	"MOEM"
One liner	"MOEM"
"MOEM"	One liner
One liner	"MOEM"

Shared/Interactive Writing

Our increasingly digital world is a wonderful place to practice shared writing. Traditional approaches to shared/interactive writing can be transfered to the interactive whiteboard, as students contribute to writing pieces as a whole class, concentrating on skills such as spelling, high-frequency–word recognition, punctuation, and composing. The interactive whiteboard is more powerful than a piece of chart paper because the work can be saved and revisited or linked to pictures, videos, or games that further support students as they write together.

Food

The cold deserts have lots of food. Goats live in some cold deserts so we can have cheese and them. We could cut the cheese with our knife. It is hard for plants-to to grow. Kit fox's, kangaroo rats, rabbits, birds, camel's thorn, sheep, mountain goats, gazelle, gerbils, wolves and lama/camels for meat. We could cu-t open there stomach and take out the inside so we don't get sick. This is one of the main things you need to survive.

Water

Water is not easy to find in the deseclean water rt, but the Saxaul tree does stor es water in its bark. It only rains an average 15-26 cm of rain per year in most cold deserts. We could use are rain coat for that. Camels store water in their humps. There are many small lakes in the cold deserts and we can bathe, drink and catch small fish-in them. We can cut open a cactus with the swiss army knife and drink some of its juice and store the rest in the water bottle for later.

See Chapter 5 for more suggestions about creating with social action.

Another important writing experience is using social media for social action, and students can be exposed to this experience very early in school. As students write using social media, their peers and others instantly respond and comment, creating a dialogue and expanding the writing piece. Writing can be more authentic and purposeful, as students can use shared writing to address issues: e.g., Tweet to the principal or a local politician about an issue, such as an unsafe play structure at the park; participate in shared writing on a blog about deforestation; or compose an e-mail to pen pals across the globe. These practices are motivating for students and engage them in authentic writing.

Traditional

When creating a shared-writing piece, one large collaborative piece of text is usually created. Either as a whole class or in small groups facilitated by a teacher, students work collaboratively on a piece of writing and everyone is encouraged to participate. Shared writing for social action can involve students voicing their knowledge or opinions in writing. They might brainstorm ideas and then write a letter, individually or in pairs, to a community representative or local newspaper. They mail the letter and wait for a response.

IWB Advantage

On the interactive whiteboard, students can easily participate in shared/interactive writing. The teacher can start with different types of graphic organizers that can be easily copied onto a notebook page to make organizing ideas easier for students, or existing ideas can simply be shifted into new organizers as necessary. Students can take turns adding ideas or opinions to the piece as the teacher assists, or they can use collaborative writing programs that allow them all to contribute at the same time. While students create, they can move sentences around freely, changing the mood and tone of the piece. Text can be edited by teacher or peers for the whole class or small group to see, and then changes can be accepted or reviewed. You can share the completed text by posting it on the class blog or website or by sending it as an e-mail. It can also be included in the weekly newsletter for the parents, created by their children.

An Interactive Idea for Social Action

Objective
To voice students' knowledge and opinions as they reflect on a unit on communities.

Hook
Reflect on the finished unit. Access a map of the local community on the IWB and ask students to identify important aspects of their community, using the pens to circle and label.

Lesson
1. After looking at the characteristics of a community, critically look at one aspect of the community that could be changed to improve the living space for everyone. This could include the amount of park space, accessibility, or traffic congestion. Using the IWB, students can flip between map and satellite views of a community to analyze the amount of green space, the landforms, and how these things relate to the location of the buildings.
2. Students pick a topic they are passionate about and create a list of practical suggestions for improvement. Peers can add to the list by accessing the document when they visit the IWB in small groups. They can move suggestions around, with the idea at the top being the most realistic and the one at the bottom the least realistic.
3. Take one example and model writing a letter to the appropriate community representative. This modeled writing can be saved on another slide and students can access it by splitting the screen when they compose their own letters. Completed letters can be mailed or e-mailed. Letters can be posted directly on a blog for a newspaper article or local community organizations that address the same issue.

Closure
If you choose to post the letter publicly, then link as a whole class to the website periodically to see if anyone has added comments. By publicly posting letters, your chances to receive feedback has increased and your students will see that their opinions have been shared.

Independent Writing

We provide our literacy lessons—modeled, shared, and guided—to build a base of skills for our students, so that when students write independently they have the skills and knowledge to successfully complete independent activities. Using the interactive whiteboard, we can guide them through writing their name, putting words into sentences, and creating meaningful text in multiple paragraphs. The large canvas of the IWB instantly creates two possibilities:

1. It is a safe space to interact, play, and manipulate writing so that, when writing is complete, students can understand and read back their text. Students can write and use features such as Recognize to provide feedback to them about the clarity of their writing. They can manipulate their words by moving them around and rearranging sentences. The easy manipulation allows them to play with words and letters to help form their ideas.

This screenshot shows a sentence-writing activity that was a literacy centre for Grade 1 students. In small groups, students dragged cloned words and used the pens to independently create new sentences and edit them collaboratively.

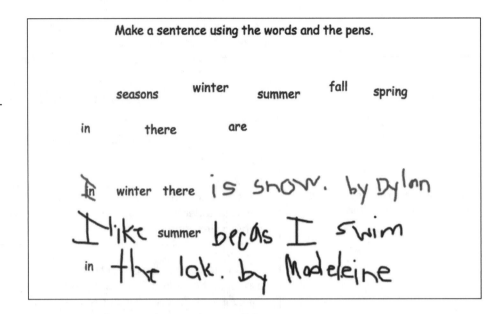

Make a sentence using the words and the pens.

seasons   winter   summer   fall   spring

in   there   are

In winter there is snow. by Dylan

I like summer becas I swim in the lak. by Madeleine

2. The large space also provides a forum for instant publishing. The sheer size of the IWB acts as a bulletin board for students to share their writing. They can copy and paste their newly formed text onto a page in a class book, onto their own book, onto an e-mail, or even onto a blog.

Valuing Linguistic Differences

Identity Texts

Refer to the work of Jim Cummins or visit www.multiliteracies.ca to learn more about identity texts.

One powerful example of integrating student identities, valuing cultural and linguistic diversity, and integrating technology into writing instruction is through identity texts. Working collaboratively with teachers, parents, and peers—as well as accessing resources (e.g., online translators)through the IWB—students of all ages can author individual books written in two languages; i.e., English and their first languages. Books can be illustrated by the student author or images can be transported into the book from the computer. Books can be burned to DVD and mailed to family members in home countries; they can be posted online and sent via e-mail; or a site can be set up for parents and family members to access these books.

In this screenshot, a student created an identity text to share with his class. His language became an important part of the class and his own invented text.

I love to go to school. It is so fun to learn new things. I also love to see my friends everyday at school.

אני אוהב ללך לבית ספר. זה מאד קף ללמוד דברים חדשים. אני גם אוהב לראות את החברים שלי כל יום בבית ספר.

Second/Added Language Learning

Being a literate learner means moving fluidly through disciplines and incorporating listening, speaking, reading, and writing skills into various subjects, be it math, science, art, or history. Many schools, districts, and governments mandate a second language in the curriculum. Second-language programs increasingly use gestures, manipulatives, or games to enhance understanding. The interactive whiteboard is yet another tool that can help students gain access to another language. Using the interactive whiteboard, you can help support second-language learning by

- Accessing online websites and games for students to play, such as games with Flash players that incorporate sound. Games could support everything from matching vocabulary, to learning verb phrases, to listening and responding to longer text.
- Creating interactive games. Layer graphics and text to be revealed when clicked on; or make anagram templates with visuals, text, and puzzles.

Grade 7 students were given cameras to take photos of various facial expressions. They used the photos to collaboratively create a game, using a template provided with the SMART Board. In the game, students were asked a question, given a visual clue, and then asked to unscramble the anagram to answer the question (here *la déception*, or disappointment). To add an element of competition, a timer could be used.

- Linking sounds to pictures to hear the words pronounced accurately and in different voices.
- Using applications or Web 2.0 tools for students to create movies or presentations using the second language. Creating an advertisement or commercial for a product in a second language is an engaging way to incorporate visuals, oral language, and text.
- Creating an engaging template—such as a posting shapes and allowing the students to create a picture using the shapes, pens, and tools. Require that students speak only the second language to explain their next step.

In this screenshot, the use of visual cues and written text is being modeled for the Kindergarten class of teacher Guillaume Dupre as they listen for and read rhymes in a second language. *What should they be looking for when creating a match? What should they hear?* They follow up by playing the game with manipulatives and orally recreating the sounds.

Image taken from *Jeu de'association – Je fais de rimes* produced by The Learning Journey International, LLC. © All rights reserved.

Traditional

Students learning a second language have descriptive words listed on a chart or whiteboard for future reference. Students refer to the list to try to incorporate new vocabulary into oral or written tasks. They can hear the words used in context in a sentence or have the words read to them from a storybook or text. Sometimes the new words in the second language are translated, or a visual is drawn beside the new word to support meaning making.

IWB Advantage

Using the IWB, students can collectively brainstorm appropriate word choices, make errors and fix them easily, and move words into created categories. They can add graphics and other visual cues (such as using different pen colors for parts of speech) to words. They can click on a word and have it pronounced for them by the IWB, thereby creating an audio link to the words. You can group words on each document so that students can click on the "transportation" page to recall the specific word they are looking for. Words can be easily added.

An Interactive Idea for Learning French Vocabulary

Objective

To speak confidently in French, incorporating descriptive vocabulary to describe an object in history. This lesson is cross-curricular, as it connects to prior knowledge from a social studies unit.

Hook

- Tell the students the topic for discussion: What type of boat did the explorers use when first coming to Canada? Display graphics of different types of boats (a sailboat, a yacht, a speedboat, a rowboat, a pirate ship) and have the students use the IWB pens to cross out the ones they think would be improbable. During independent work time, have students use the IWB pen to sign their names under the boat they think is a probable choice.
- Brainstorm descriptive words with students as they refer to the visual displayed on the IWB. Have them record the words randomly on the IWB. As a class, group the words into themes by moving them around on the IWB.

Lesson

1. Divide the class into groups. Each group will have the opportunity to work together at the IWB. Other groups can be engaged in other small-group tasks.
2. Post a blank template on the board. Explain to students that they are responsible for creating a picture of a boat French explorers might have used in the 1800s. They must
- Communicate only in French
- Use the brainstormed vocabulary to justify their drawing of the boat (using either shapes or pens)
- Search for images if necessary to communicate their ideas
- Take equal turns
3. You can facilitate the activity by prompting, using short questions in French. You might also circulate and listen to the students as they use descriptive words to plan and create their structure.

Closure

Ask the group to take a screenshot of their product. Have students transfer the screenshot onto a blank template and add lines for writing. Print the template; it becomes an individual writing task for which students add their own thoughts about the product they created, using descriptive words.

2

Using the Interactive Whiteboard

In the same way we gain confidence using any new tool, use of the interactive whiteboard will have a learning curve.

The applications outlined in this chapter are available on most interactive whiteboards. However, they are accessed in a variety of ways, depending on the type of IWB being used. For specifics on how to use these applications for the first time, we suggest opening the software and playing with it.

So, you have this rather expensive, fancy interactive whiteboard in your classroom. Now what? Many teachers are intimidated by the IWB because they don't know where to start. Think of the interactive whiteboard as a classroom tool, just as chalk, pens, pencils, and overheads are well-loved classroom tools. We probably couldn't imagine our classroom without pencils, a black/white board, paper, and books. Once you are comfortable with your interactive whiteboard, it will be difficult to imagine the classroom without one.

This chapter will walk through the basic features available on common interactive whiteboards. We begin with the notion that *whatever can be done on a computer, can be done on an interactive whiteboard.* As you work through the basics and become more comfortable with the interactive features, you will imagine many uses for the IWB. Ultimately, it is in the aspects of collaborative community and interactive learning that the interactive whiteboard excels. Your IWB will evolve as you use it, and you yourself will be part of the learning process as you gain confidence using it. As with all technology, as you stumble through the mechanics, your students will analyze, brainstorm, experiment, problem solve, and eventually become your partners in learning its capabilities.

Interacting with a Blank Document

Most interactive whiteboards come with their own software. By opening the software and selecting either a blank page or chart paper, you instantly create a blank document that you can interact with in a variety of ways:
- Blank documents become the canvas for your lessons.
- You can add drawings, words, and graphics by using pens, saved files, images from the Internet, and the keyboard.
- You can drag and drop a backdrop for the document, such as writing paper or a map of the world, and color fill with the tool bar.
- You can access pre-created graphics and interactive lessons from a variety of sources, such as the IWB gallery/library and online repositories where teachers share resources.
- Anything you add to this blank document can be moved and altered (by changing size, orientation, color, etc.). It is important to understand this so that the IWB remains interactive for your students

Using blank documents, you can save information, come back to it later and continue to add to, delete, move, and shift what you previously thought. Learning and teaching are open to continual reflection and growth.

Organizing Documents

Once you have added information to a document, as with any digital file, you want to save it. You can organize a file by saving each document in the file with the key concept. You can choose to save documents individually or group them together under one concept. The file can now be easily accessed by a keyword search. Your students can reference information from previous lessons by glancing through the key concepts. You can also display all the key concepts that have been covered at a quick glance. This organizational system, along with the interactive markings from your students, displays what has been covered and can easily be accessed for review.

This screenshot shows the organization of a unit on the sun on a SMART Board. Each group of pages is saved under a key concept. This provides structure and acts a quick reference for students as well as the teacher.

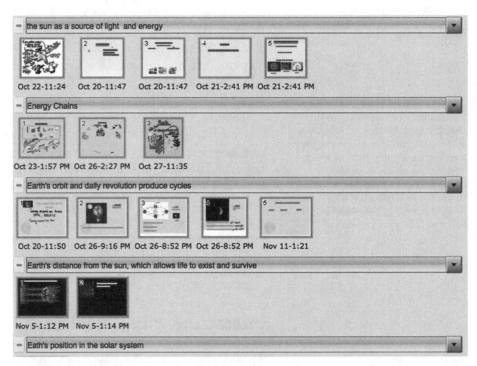

Interacting with Ink: IWB Pens

Throughout history, one of the simplest and most interactive items has been the pen. The pen has evolved from feather quill to fountain pen to ballpoint—and now to a piece of technology that directly writes on an interactive screen. Once a student picks up a pen and writes on the interactive whiteboard, that student is using a meaningful digital tool.

Using an IWB pen, students can interact with a document visually, digitally, and in a written format. The pens can write over anything displayed on the interactive whiteboard, such as movies, pictures, and text; they can highlight, circle, and draw attention to details; they can move ideas and join words. Once an image or unit of text (word, sentence, etc.) is on the IWB, it becomes a piece of digital text that needs only the touch of a pen to alter color, font, shape, orientation, and size. Using the pens on the interactive whiteboard holds many possibilities:

- With the backdrop of a news website, students can circle contrasting statements or opinions vs. facts, and critically write over the piece to display their thoughts.

- While a movie is shown on the IWB, students can circle an area of interest and watch specifically for the impact of that one section, such as a mysterious door in a mystery drama.
- With the backdrop of a map, students can plot out where a city should be built and then design and draw the roadway systems.
- With a blank template of a mind map, students can write their ideas, come back later and add more, rearrange thoughts, delete irrelevant information, and link connecting ideas.

In these screenshots, the teacher created a template for students to use to add their newfound knowledge through several lessons using the SMART Board pens. Over the course of a week, small groups of students collaborated to click and move ideas from one spot to another. They clicked on the link to access a video about rocks (courtesy of Mark Owen) and they added ideas, and linked to and expanded on previous thoughts.

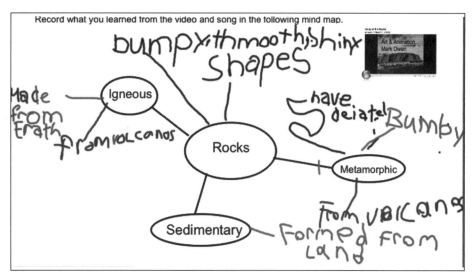

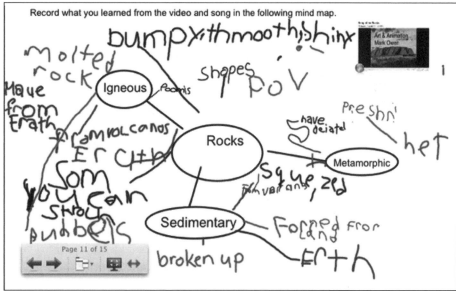

Quick Pen Tricks

Calibrating

To ensure your interactive whiteboard is aligned properly, touch the pen to the screen. If the arrow and the tip of the pen do not touch, the board needs to be realigned. Each kind of IWB has its own quick shortcuts to access calibration. Once the screen starts producing a set of crossing lines (one at a time), the calibration is being done. Using the finest point possible (the tip of a pen rather than a finger) provides a more accurate response. When the screen is calibrated, the arrow and the pen will directly align.

Finger Writing

With some IWBs, once the pen is selected for use (or removed from the tray), anything can be used to write. Young children struggling with fine motor skills can use larger objects or a finger. If the IWB software is open, you can select the thickness of the ink and adjust features, such as the color. The pens need to be back in position in the tray (or the arrow selected) to stop this feature.

Erasing

Newer IWBs use a pen to write. By holding and moving your fist on the board, you can erase. Some IWBs have an eraser in the holding tray with the pens. In older versions, accessing the tool kit provides an eraser. You can choose the thickness to determine the impact.

Recognizing

Once you have written something, it becomes a piece of digital text. When you click on the word, a menu bar of options will appear. One option is to Recognize the word and change the writing into a computer font. This is a useful tool for primary students. It offers instant feedback for their print formation and spelling.

Saving

For more detailed instructions on saving a screenshot, check your IWB manual. Tips might also be available online.

Once you have written on a piece of work (such as a website, movie, or other piece of software), the interactive whiteboard recognizes this action and will open and offer the chance to save your work. You can skip this option by erasing the marks completely. If the pen markings are not fully erased, the option to save will pop up when you try to move the work. This will instantly open the IWB software and save a digital picture of the screen. Just as with paper, we choose what to do with our work; we can toss it in the trash or keep it.

Taking a screenshot of the work (or a camera image of selected work) is a simple way to instantly save what has been completed. Once students have mastered this skill, it can act as instant record for assessment. You can print the file, drag it into the student's folder, or share it immediately. Interacting with screenshots can instantly change how you teach and assess:

- You can take screenshots of a modeled assignment and post in on the class website or blog for students to access outside of the classroom.
- You can take a screenshot of a class project to e-mail directly to the principal or parents for support.
- The class can collaboratively create the monthly calendar, then take a screenshot and e-mail it to parents.
- Students can select the exact point where they feel their work is complete and save it. They can take a photo of it and neatly store it on the desktop for easy access.
- Once a group has completed a task and taken the screenshot, you can put a copy in each student's digital portfolio folder. The file lives and develops as your students' learning grows throughout the unit, or year.

See Chapter 6 for more on the use of clickers for assessment.

Using Clickers

There are various additional tools that accompany the interactive whiteboard, depending on the brand. The Learner Response System, or clickers, is a tool developed for most IWBs and many projector systems. The system consists of a clicker, or handheld receiver, for each student and design software incorporated in the programs. You can create quizzes, tests, or anything that requires a selected response. Using the accompanying program, you can design questionnaires involving multiple-choice, multiple-answer, true-and-false, and yes-and-no questions. When the question is posted, students respond immediately. The clickers record who responded and if the answers were accurate. They tally total scores and give a breakdown about specific questions. You can use this information to determine who understands the concept and who needs more assistance.

Interacting with the Basic Toolbar

The interactive whiteboard software houses a toolbar to access a variety of resources to enhance lessons and enable student interaction. With the toolbar, you can
- Open a new document, save the current document, delete a document, and flip though the documents in the file easily.
- Undo, redo, copy, paste, and delete text.
- Click on the whole screen so that only the work on the program in use is displayed.
- Display two screens at once so that information can be easily moved.
- Shade or hide part of the screen, so that information can be revealed easily.
- Drag and drop a variety of simple geometric shapes and lines to add a visual element to documents.
- Alter the background color fill, text shape, size, or color, or change the ink on the pens.
- Insert charts.
- Highlight information using a highlighter.
- Access a keyboard to type in website addresses, interact with Internet games, or add typing to documents.

Options for Interaction

In addition to the basic toolbar, the interactive whiteboard software also comes equipped with a gallery or library. Once we open the gallery or library, we are presented with three options.

1. Accessing Interactive Multimedia for Lessons

The gallery/library offers various interactive tools for classroom use. Each of these tools can be dragged and dropped onto the document. Once they are on the document, you can enlarge or shrink the tool. With a quick search, you can find many still images and animated graphics and tools that enhance classroom learning:
- Use a large classroom calculator to model calculator use, or have the students experiment by interacting with the calculator on the IWB.
- Post a timer for a speed drill or to chunk a task for a group of individuals.

- Use tools that convert between imperial and metric notation (rulers, thermometers, etc.).
- Post numbers, letters, and words that have sound attached for pronunciation.
- Add a numerical or letter die to transform a lesson into a game.
- Have students create a band with musical instruments.
- Have students interact with models of the human body to see how systems move and integrate.
- Post a hundreds chart and enter a number to highlight number patterns.
- Simply drag and drop pre-created tutorials, such as lessons on food chains, parts of a plant, grammar, gravity, animated stories, how to write letters.

2. Accessing Templates or Files to Support Teaching

Within the gallery/library there are pre-created templates to use. You can build interactive activities for students using preformed templates:
- Language games: anagrams, category sort, sentence arrange, revealing templates, word guessing.
- Questioning templates: multiple choice, yes/no, true or false, multiple answer.
- Image games: memory, puzzles, world maps, timelines, image sorting, arranging and matching.

3. Accessing Online Lessons and Support

With a simple click on the gallery or library, you can directly link to your IWB's website. Within each of the main websites is a large bank of pre-created lessons that be easily downloaded and instantly used. Lessons can be sorted by grade level or topic, or can be searched using keywords. Prior to beginning a lesson on a common topic, search the bank. Pre-created templates can also be downloaded, easily altered, and saved to suit the needs of your students. Finally, these websites welcome teacher submissions. You can upload your favorite lessons to share with colleagues around the world.

Interacting with Graphics

Graphics or visual images alter how we read information and are, in fact, texts themselves. They can enhance comprehension of print text by adding visual cues or they can be a source of information on their own. Incorporating graphics into documents can be done in a variety of ways:
- Use the gallery/library and select from a bank of pre-created graphics.
- Drag and drop graphics from online sources.
- Create your own graphics with the toolbar and pens.

In this screenshot, the students worked collaboratively to create a picture of a strong structure using shapes from the SMART Board. They needed to discuss the design and take turns adding to the graphic. Using the interactive whiteboard, they could easily shift and alter their ideas as they progressed.

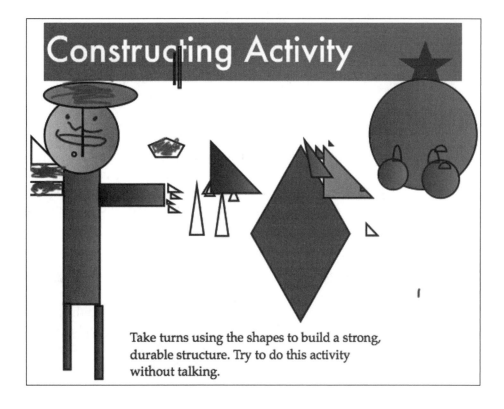

Quick Tricks with Graphics

Linking

You can link to an external source, such as a web page or online source. You can also link internally to another file in the document or another file in your computer.

Anything created on your document can be linked to a variety of sources, such as a movie, a game, or another web page. By linking a graphic, we attach to it a "link" to another place; when we click on it, we are instantly taken to that other place. The original document remains in the background. Anything on the document can be linked, such as a written word or a graphic.

To an Online Source
- Using this feature, students can link to a movie, watch it, and then come back to write down what they have learned on a graphic organizer. Even young students quickly grasp how to fluidly move through the various screens.
- Students can link to games. Teachers can set up games and provide students with links so that, when they have completed other work on the IWB or when they have answered a question correctly, the feedback can be a link to a fun activity.
- Students can access models when creating their own work. If creating a class website, you can link to a few strong examples of other websites to provide references. Students can click on the link to see an example and then return to their document to continue working on their task.

To Another Page in the File
- These links provide a valuable quick reference for students and teachers. Students can easily return to the document listing the main concepts or work in progress.
- Linking documents in the file also creates the template for games or the Language Centres described in Chapter 3. Once you have created a main document page, you can link other pages to it to connect learning. For instance,

if the main page is scattered with images that link to other pages in the document, then students can just click on an image and it will show other documents containing questions, ideas, or tasks. Students can use the main document to keep linking to other documents in the file that relate to the work they are learning about.

To Any File on the Computer
- You can easily link to and post a worksheet created in another program, high-light key words, or use the pens to model various responses.
- You can link to presentation software, such as a movie-making program, and model how to use it. You can take screenshots of the steps to complete a task and then post these steps and have the students arrange them in order.

Cloning

Cloning is sometimes referred to as "infinite cloning."

Cloning allows you to make multiple identical copies of the graphic, text, or document you are working on.

You can set up an activity and then clone a copy for each group of students. You can also clone text or a graphic in the document. Unlimited copies provide students with more confidence, as they can work though numbers or letters or graphics, experimenting, moving, deleting, and ultimately creating their response to the task. A quick screenshot of each task also acts a digital record of their work. Making copies can be useful for

- Cloning the letters in a word and having students create as many words as possible, by dragging the letters down. If the letters do not make a real word, the experimental word is easy to delete. If students are unsure of spelling, they can drag the letters down and move them around easily until they agree on the spelling of the word.
- Cloning numbers and signs and having students drag to create equations.

In this screenshot, the fractions and signs are cloned. This allows the students to simply drag the numbers and symbols to complete the task.

Use the fractions to create equations that are true.

$$\frac{1}{2} \qquad \frac{1}{3} \qquad \frac{2}{3} \qquad \frac{4}{5} \qquad \frac{1}{4} \qquad \frac{3}{5} \qquad = \quad + \quad - \quad < \quad >$$

$$\frac{1}{2} < \frac{4}{5}$$

$$\frac{1}{4} + \frac{1}{4} = \frac{1}{2}$$

- Cloning graphics of pond animals and having students drag to create food chains using the animals in different arrangements.
- Cloning the elements (i.e., hydrogen, carbon) and having students drag down the appropriate amount of each element to make molecules.

Once a piece of digital text is created, either by using the pens or a as graphic, it can be layered on top of other pieces of digital text on the IWB. By layering digital text, you can create a rich experience for your students. Ordering can be accessed through the tool bar or with a click once the digital text has been selected, allowing you to place it in the background, on top, underneath another object, or resting on all objects. To remove a top layer, you can use the eraser or set it up to disappear with a click. Ordering text presents many options:

- You can place an internal diagram of the circulatory system below a picture of a person (or a student). Students can use the eraser or magnifying glass (depending on the type of IWB) to erase the top image and discover the one below.
- Quotes or favorite classroom memories can be placed below photos of students for parent nights, where parents can click on the image of their child to see what that student enjoys about school.
- Answers to questions can be placed below shapes or graphics, to be revealed when the overlying image is erased or clicked on.
- You can create guided lessons with certain information hidden until other information has been exposed.
- Screenshots of celebrated work can hide behind the balloon attendance (see page 44). When students arrive at class, they can find their names and then celebrate their learning.

Screen Sharing

The interactive whiteboard can show exactly what is on your computer screen. In many ways, this can be a useful tool. It allows you to work alongside students, touching, moving, and learning together. However, there will be times when your students are working on the interactive whiteboard and you need access to your computer. In these situations, you can access screen displays and "turn off mirroring" so that students view or work on the interactive whiteboard while you work on your computer screen without students being able to see what is there.

Interacting with Movies

See Chapter 4 for more on interacting with movies.

There are two main ways to show movies on the interactive whiteboard. You can connect a separate DVD or VHS player to the IWB and show the movie directly. When using this option, you use the IWB remote control to select the source that will be displayed on the IWB.

As an alternative, you can insert the DVD into the computer, using the IWB to show what is playing on the computer. By choosing to show the movie directly from the computer, you can

- Access the IWB software, allowing you to make connections with the movie and the previously taught lesson.
- Take screenshots of various points in the movie for later activities.

- Pause the movie and write on the screen with the pens to highlight important concepts.
- Flip between the movie and a worksheet that accompanies the movie to model filling it in using pens.
- Show online movies and clips.

Interacting with Other Sources

Anything that can be used on the computer can be used by students and teachers together on the interactive whiteboard. One advantage of the IWB is that you need to purchase only one piece of software for an entire class to use. With a license for one piece of software, you can

- Use a graphing program to take attendance, one that easily converts between pie charts, bar charts, and pictographs.
- Use a graphic organizer program for small-group work or whole-class lessons to reflect on taught concepts.
- Use map websites for geography lessons, planning a community, or studying earth sciences.
- Use a calendar program to mark the days of school and perform morning routines.
- Use premade templates that students can move around easily, such as base 10 blocks.

The Internet is a wonderful source for free programs. By linking to an Internet browser, you can

- Post the local weather network for the weather routine.
- Bookmark a variety of interactive games for early finishers or for skill practice.
- Perform the same search on a variety of browsers to see what different websites are posted.
- Open a blog for a "hot topic" in the classroom and review previously posted comments. Using the pens, students can circle comments that either support or counter what has been discussed. They can form a class opinion and use the keyboard to share that perspective. Bookmark the blog to revisit it later and see how the conversation progresses.
- Post the Twitter page of a person of interest (local politician or favorite author) to review previous comments this person has made. Students can use the pens to mark key comments that demonstrate their opinions. Have the students create a character sketch of this person, using the Tweets as a source for the points they make. Find an article on the person online. How does the students' character sketch differ from the one in the media portal? How can people use Twitter to shape their identity?

This series of screenshots shows math challenges that teacher Meg Davies gave to her students to begin class each day for three days. To work through these problems, the students were linked to data from the government's census website. They used authentic data to work though math equations, critically thinking about the implications. The SMART Board supported this learning, as the students fluidly flipped from the task to the websites, copying and pasting data and moving it around to form order. Their work was then saved and cloned so that the students could complete the next task the following day with the same data, changing the order. The easy dragging and placing of information made this complex task manageable and allowed students to critically think about their math and the real-life implications of the information.

One of the provincial responsibilities is healthcare. However, it is such a big responsibility, that sometimes the federal government helps out.

The federal government currently gives healthcare transfer payments to provincial governments based on provincial population.

Using the data given, put the provinces in order from who will get the most federal transfer funds to who will get the least.

There is a debate right now as to whether basing the transfer payments on population is fair. What if one province has many more unhealthy people living there?

Using the data given, put the provinces in order from who will get the most federal transfer funds to who will get the least, based on one of the health based factors.

There is a debate right now as to whether basing the transfer payments on population is fair. What if one province has many more unhealthy people living there?

Challenge:

If the federal government is giving out 2.4 billion dollars, how much will each province get, based on population?

what if they base it on another factor?

Using Information from Other Sources

In many ways, the Internet is an endless and unlimited source of information. We can access information on many topics. However, there are laws surrounding what we can reproduce and use in our own classrooms. Therefore, teachers need to be aware of the following:

- Most material available on the Internet is protected by copyright. Therefore, when accessing text (e-mail messages, images, photographs, video clips, etc.), you may not reproduce, distribute, or use material from the Internet without permission from the owner.
- Copyright specifically protects information and how it is expressed. The actual information is not protected by copyright. Students and teachers can restate ideas, facts, or information in their own words and this is not a copyright infringement. However, proper citation of sources is required.
- In Canada and the United States, the Access Copyright licence allows teachers to copy up to 10 per cent of a work for use in teaching. Teachers or students can copy more than 10 per cent in the following circumstances:
  - An entire chapter that constitutes 20 per cent or less of a book.
  - An entire single short story, play, essay, or poem from a book, periodical, or anthology.
  - An entire newspaper article or page.
  - An entry from a reference work.
  - An illustration or photograph from a publication containing other works.

For more detailed information about legally accessing information, please consult *Copyright Matters: Some key questions and answers for teachers*.

3 Collaborating

Education has changed. The old view of a classroom filled with students sitting quietly at their desks, with the teacher as authority and holder of knowledge, handing out photocopied sheets of uniform work, no longer meets the needs of our students. Now we know much more about how students learn, and our teaching must be a response to that. One of the biggest changes in education is the concept of collaboration and what that means in the classroom. A collaborative activity is one in which the participants must share and negotiate to solve problems and complete tasks. This group knowledge and experience then helps them form and develop their own ideas.

Primary students love to collaborate with others in the classroom by showing and sharing. They often visit the teacher to show what they have made or found, or just to talk about ideas they have and to get feedback or reinforcement for a job well done or a good idea. They do this with peers too, calling classmates over to "look" or moving into groups to see what others are doing. As students get older, social talk is a dominant text in the classroom, as students work through ideas together and share their thinking. They answer complex questions, solve problems, and interact using rich dialogue while collaborating.

On the most basic level, the single- or multi-touch aspect of the IWB requires students to communicate and collaborate. They need to talk to each other in order to complete any group activity, to ensure that the IWB follows their direction and that they receive the feedback or meet the learning goals they are striving to achieve. The interactive whiteboard can support collaboration by making it possible to archive work to be revisited and shared later, or by providing opportunities for feedback that can be given in the form of reinforcement for activities completed.

The interactive whiteboard is also a tool that allows students to collaborate on many more levels in large and small groups in the classroom. Students can work together using the digital tools available on the interactive whiteboard to

- View common images or watch video.
- Store ideas and questions on a new unit or topic. Ideas can then be moved, sorted, and marked up as the students gain a stronger understanding of the information.
- Respond to questions posted by the teacher or each other and then receive feedback by accessing links set up by the teacher.
- Investigate Internet links or play interactive games set up by the teacher.
- Collaboratively create movies using multicultural or multilingual characters. With Junior/Intermediate students, this is a wonderful way for students to talk and produce a product that demonstrates higher-level thinking skills. The theme of the movies can be assigned based on content being explored in class.

The first step in setting up students for success as they collaborate in the classroom is to organize effectively for both large and small groups to work together, and to provide meaningful activities to support that.

Organizing for Collaboration: Incorporating the Social

Research tells us that students learn best when they have the opportunity to engage in social interactions with teachers and peers that

- Guide their learning.
- Allow for social language that gives them the opportunity to express ideas, negotiate, and problem solve.
- Are guided by high-level questions that encourage critical thinking.

Understanding your class dynamic, how students collaborate and interact, has impact on how your classroom operates. When you look at your class as a whole, the range students present in terms of ability, interest, motivation, and enthusiasm toward a given idea guides your teaching. The dynamic of how your students interact with each other and with you also affects how you set up your classroom and create lessons. Some ways to incorporate a social-learning philosophy are to

- Group your students in various ways: heterogeneous groups for some types of learning and homogeneous groups for others.
- Use paired work for some tasks: i.e., using "think, pair, share" when students are required to answer questions; or grouping students in pairs for problem-solving tasks.
- Encourage talk in your classroom as students work through learning tasks.
- Use the IWB to allow students to participate in social groupings with other classes in other schools or with their families.

Traditional

A traditional K–4 classroom is structured in a number of ways: students choose partners, partners are assigned (either by naming partners or by proximity in a seating plan), or groups are formed for a given task. These groups are either heterogeneous (stronger/weaker students together), homogeneous (like students together), or random. Students generally stay together in groups for long periods of time; for example, when teachers form reading groups for small-group reading instruction.

IWB Advantage

Just as we can interact with information on the IWB, the structure of student groupings can also be interactive when an IWB is used. One idea is to simply post a table on the IWB and explain to the students that they need to work with a variety of people (never the same person twice). They can sign in and complete assigned activities with various partners, rotating through their own created groups. As students progress through the activities, they select new partners by moving the names around, yet still displaying the previous partnership by cloning their names. They can track who they have worked with and see who they still need to work with.

An Interactive Idea for Collaboration

Objective
To provide opportunities for students to interact with classmates and to collaborate in a safe environment.

Hook
Share a quick video clip on the IWB showing the earth's rotation around the sun and highlighting the seasons. Set up a link on the word for each season. The link will take the students to a graphic that represents that season. As each season is displayed, have a student drag the word into the top row of a table set up on the IWB. You may want to take a screenshot of the graphic for each season as a visual display for the lesson, especially in the earlier grades.

Lesson
1. Each student gets a different partner for each of the four seasons. The partners can be arranged heterogeneously or homogeneously.
2. Set up a chart like the one below and display it on the IWB. When you call out "Summer partners," students work in that grouping for a given activity.
3. Throughout the year, students are provided with many possibilities to interact with different peers in the class. Here is a sample rotational chart with students A, B, C, D, E, F, G, and H:

Summer	Spring	Fall	Winter
A & B	A & C	A & D	A & F
C & D	B & E	E & H	B & C
E & F	D & G	B & G	D & H
G & H	H & F	F & C	C & G

4. At various points, when students need to be paired up for tasks or just in talk partners, the students work in seasonal partners. At the end of the task or activity, the students will have worked with a variety of peers. The same idea can be used with groups. The partner pairings shown in the table can be dragged into group formations and displayed on the IWB: e.g. drag A & B together with E & F for a group activity. Groupings can be changed simply by dragging different combinations from the table together. Students can participate in the formation of groups.

Closure
Change the seasonal partners each term. Periodically give students a chance to reflect on their experiences by posting a link on the partner display to a private self/peer evaluation. Have the students work in their seasonal partners to consider questions like these: Which peers did they find supportive to work with? Which peers would be good to work with again? Why did they think that combination was successful? Students and teachers can later refer to this information when arranging groupings.

Whole-Class Organization

The interactive whiteboard can function as a way to organize the classroom community. It can be a work board, directing students to tasks and expectations for various centres. It can allow students to sign-in for various activities and track when they or their group has completed those activities. It can provide space for students to give feedback on activities completed. It allows students to call up past activities and add to them as a group, or use them as anchors for future work. It can even be used as a behavioral management tool, to set goals (e.g., number of students ready after one prompt) and to track individual or group progress toward the goal on a chart or graph. Using the IWB as a tool to organize your class, you can create meaningful ways of tracking your students that are also engaging and motivating.

The interactive whiteboard is an effective tool for classroom organization, either though tracking of individuals, small groups, or the entire class. Once you have created the template for your class organizational system, then you can save it and easily access it for the next assignment or for future years. Although the initial creation of your templates can take time, using the IWB can result in significant savings in terms of, for example, index cards and library pockets; it lets you avoid the problem of missing name cards, ripped library pockets, and fading bulletin boards. The digital aspect of the IWB allows you to directly save both your work and students' work in simple, easy-to-access computer files. The information in the files can be saved, modified, and infinitely cloned to provide you with more flexibility and options in the organization of your classroom.

Attendance Routines

Even routines don't exist in a vacuum but provide opportunities for students' literacy learning, mathematics, and gaining knowledge about the world around them. Just by using the interactive whiteboard to change the approach to a common classroom routine, such as taking attendance, you can expand the possibilities for learning:

• You can use a template, such as Balloon Pop on a SMART Board, to post the names of your students. As students arrive, they pop the balloon with their name, encouraging name recognition.

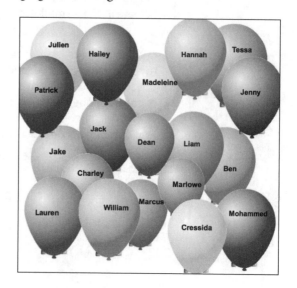

- Students learning to write or struggling with grip can use a finger or a manipulative to write their names as they arrive.
- Clone the alphabet and have students practice recognizing and selecting the letter that their name starts with for their attendance. They can move the letter into the position of the first letter, thereby completing a cloze activity. This can progress into selecting all the letters of their name sequentially.
- Students who can write can sign their names on the IWB in a square or circle that is made progressively smaller. The students can size the shape themselves by pressing on the shape to make it bigger or smaller.
- On arrival students can add their names to the board and sort their own name in alphabetical order (moving the other names to make room).
- You can incorporate a Venn diagram or other graphic organizer to prompt the morning conversation/community circle. Set up sections with words such as "excited," happy," "OK," or "tired." As students arrive, they can drag their names to the appropriate section, prompting a morning conversation about feelings.

As students arrived in the classroom, they clicked on a dropdown menu with a variety of options of how they felt about the upcoming unit. Using InspireData® and the touch screen, this data was converted into a bar graph and then a pie graph.

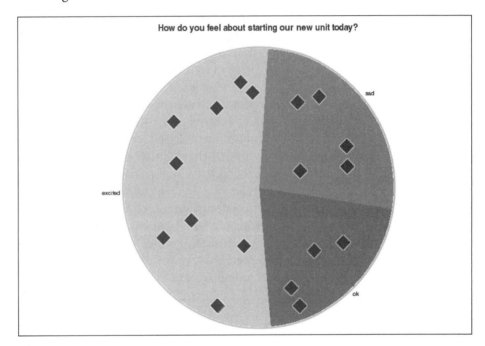

How do you feel about starting our new unit today?

sad

excited

ok

- Post a question related to the previous lesson, such as "Which explorer do you think had the biggest impact on our culture?" Using a graphing program, you can provide a dropdown menu. This data can be converted into a graph and you can then use this data as a discussion prompt.

As the year progresses, students will develop their ability to write and print on the interactive whiteboard. Once a student is able to write his or her name, they can use the Recognize tool to convert the printing into a typed font. But students need to write neatly and keep the pen connected to the letter on the board to be successful. Many students consider an accurate "recognized" word a successfully written word. This tool provides students with the instant feedback about spelling that they desire when learning to write. As well, saving copies of the attendance sign-in screens throughout the year creates an assessment tool you can use to monitor the progress of your students' letter recognition and letter formation. These saved screens also provide a clear showcase to track development and can be evidence of progress for a parent–teacher conference.

Managing Behavior

How our students choose to behave directly affects what they may learn or achieve at any given moment. Our students' behavior choices affect their peers and their opportunities for learning. As teachers, we spend a great deal of time during the day directing our students toward positive choices in behavior and learning. We all have various tricks and tools to assist us in guiding our students.

The interactive whiteboard is another tool that you can employ to assist in managing behavior. Any of the traditional wall posters that you post—on bulletin boards, traditional black/whiteboards, or the wall—can be replicated for the IWB. By making the activity interactive, you create more possibilities to record, connect, and update your behavior program. For instance:

- For positive reinforcement and goal setting, post a class list on the IWB. Every student who, for example, can put on his or her snowsuit within five minutes, can put a star beside his or her name. If there are fifteen stars before the five-minute deadline, you can flip to the next page where there is a graphic of a jar of jelly beans. Set a group objective: How long will it take for the class to fill the jar with jellybeans? Provide incentives relevant to the age group you are teaching: e.g., a homework pass for older students, a choice from the "surprise box" for younger students.
- To monitor the class behavior, post a photo of each child. Then use icons, such as green, yellow, and red lights, to provide students with a visual for positive or negative behavior choices.
- Create a template in which each student gets a personal space. Create a bank of infinitely cloned icons (both positive and negative). As students achieve a certain behavior, they can it add to their personal space. This provides instant feedback, a visual reference, and a tracking system that can be saved for later reference. To create more authentic motivation, have students select the icons to add, e.g., images of their favorite sports players or movie characters.
- Create a template of a game board where each student chooses an icon to "walk" on the game. Rather then rolling dice to move, students must demonstrate positive behaviors to move their icons along the board. You can set an individual or class goal of making it to the goal for free reading time.

In this screenshot, the gameboard and interactive die (courtesy of SMART Technologies) focus on the goal of showing respect. If a student was seen showing respect to another person or object, they would be tapped on the shoulder by a teacher or peer and they could go up to the gameboard to roll the die to move their initials. This is very effective for starting new routines and reinforcing positive behavior choices.

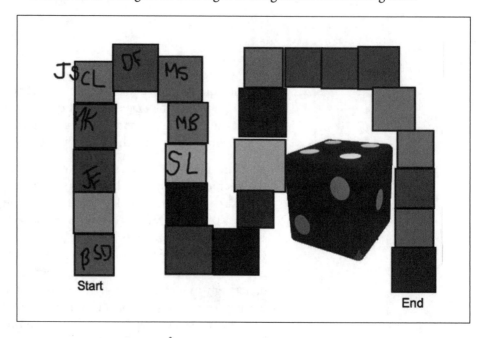

What We Find Reinforcing

When students at various grade levels were asked what they found reinforcing (O'Donnell et al., 2008), the answers differed greatly. In order for reinforcement programs to work, a carefully chosen reinforcer must be the reward. Here is what the students said:

Kindergarten Students	*Being a messenger and leaving the class on my own* *Having lunch or spending special time with the teacher in the classroom* *Receiving a special note home*
Grade 4 Students	*Computer time* *A chance to be the teacher's helper* *Homework exemption* *A chance to select the class snack*
Grade 9 Students	*Homework exemption* *Chance to retake a quiz* *Exemption from an in-class assignment*

Using the interactive whiteboard to track students' behavior creates many possibilities. You can save behavior charts on days worth noting to act as a document if a student is being monitored and you are called to give proof of behavior, either positive or negative. By pulling up saved behavior charts, you have an easy reference for formal reporting and discussions with parents. As well, the visual and interactive nature of the IWB engages students and they want to participate and to receive acknowledgment for their positive behaviors. Physically moving to touch the IWB provides energetic students a chance to move. When you use the IWB for managing class behavior you provide your students with a sense of control and engage them in a positive manner.

Independent Learning Centres

There are a variety of ways to organize your classroom, and independent learning centres offer many advantages. The interactive whiteboard is a helpful to tool to organize, maintain, track, and assess work the your students do in learning centres. It can act as a workboard for centre rotation. You can use it to track work, offer instant feedback, and save copies of completed work for assessment. Because of the large visual reference the IWB creates, students can become part of the tracking and monitoring process.

Traditional

Centres in the classroom are organized on a bulletin board. Usually centres are represented in words and pictures; e.g., the Reading Centre with a picture of a book. Students' names are printed on clothespegs, index cards, or library cards. Students have some choice in activity, or the teacher rotates small groups of students to the next activity by moving the names. Instructions for activities are posted beside the activity, printed from the computer or handwritten, or are given verbally. As with any bulletin board, this system can physically deteriorate

One of the cornerstones of a successful classroom is the use of clear and direct instructions so that all students know what they should be doing. Organizing tasks cuts down on transition time. Knowing what to do through clear expectations empowers students.

very rapidly as instructions get lost, paper rips, and names fade or fall off. This system requires a lot of teacher maintenance.

IWB Advantage

Using the IWB, you can post a chart with students' names. You can manage their tasks by creating and cloning icons for the various activities they have to complete: e.g., a graphic of a book or e-reader for reading; a large *W* for a word-work activity; a pencil or IWB pen for a writing activity. As students finish an activity, they drag the appropriate icon to a place next to their names on the chart. The chance to touch the interactive whiteboard is very motivating and helps students chart their progress. They can also see which peers have completed the other activities, encouraging a dynamic in which they can seek peer assistance.

This screeenshot shows how students tracked their task completion by dragging the dot onto the activity when it was completed. The students used this as a reference when they were stuck on a task; they knew who had completed it and who they could ask for support.

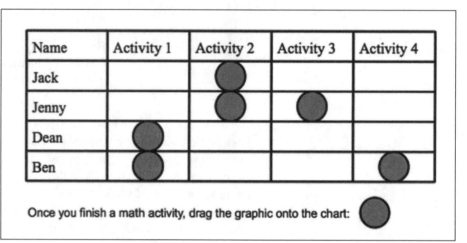

Name	Activity 1	Activity 2	Activity 3	Activity 4
Jack		●		
Jenny		●	●	
Dean	●			
Ben	●			●

Once you finish a math activity, drag the graphic onto the chart: ●

When students work directly on the IWB, they can clone the activity linked to the main work board, allowing several copies of the activity to be prepared for groups that follow. When a group completes the activity, they can save the document with their names for later assessment. The IWB also allows the students to track their own activities, knowing which they can pick from next. By watching their peers share completed work from an activity during whole-class sharing time, students can start to think about the activity and what they might like to choose for the next session.

The screenshot on page 49 shows another way to organize literacy centres during your literacy block. Divide your class into groups of four. At the start of each literacy block, have the students sit in their groups to collaborate and decide which centre they would like to visit that day. The resources available will determine the organization: one approach is to have the group select from any of the choices, but allow only one of each category to be used each day. Each activity must be simple enough so that the students understand what to do, yet complex enough to keep the students meaningfully engaged in independent practice. This organization allows small groups to work together independently, allowing the teacher to focus on a guided session with a small group.

Each group is assigned a number (as shown in the screenshot) and the number is recorded on the menu page with the activity for that day. This allows both students and teacher to track which group has completed which activities.

At the end of each unit, ask for the students' feedback and give them time to reflect on their favorite activities and why they liked them best. This information can be used when designing the next activities for the upcoming unit.

This screenshot illustrates a SMART Board sample of an organizational system for independent learning centres, with activities appropriate for K–2. Each icon links to an activity. Students work in small groups to collaboratively select their activities and track their progress. In this example, Construct is the group that works on the IWB; Compute (activity courtesy of kidspiration) is the group on the computers; Talk is the group that interacts with books and completes a task that requires them to dialogue before, during, or after reading.

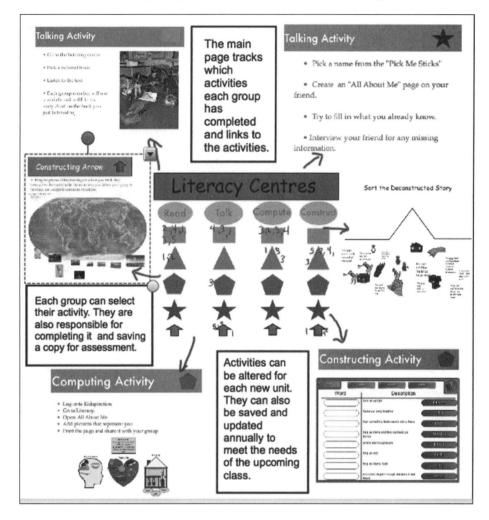

Small-Group Organization

Have you ever planned the perfect group activity? You bought the supplies, created a model, and broke the task into manageable steps; you were motivated and excited to teach it. You decided the class should work in small groups. The activity was ready and you were prepared. You modeled the task for the group and showed lots of examples. Then you sent the students off to start their small-group work. At some point, you heard, "Sam will not share," "Alexandra is not letting me play," "Charley is not helping at all." And then your heart sank. The perfectly planned activities became overtaken with negative comments and peer conflicts.

Any group activity or lesson has the possibility of failure. We have all experienced similar situations, and we have all learned tips and tricks to help make group work successful. We teach children and we know that a big part of setting them up for success is teaching them how to make good choices. It is our job to teach students what they can and should not do when considering the various options available to them. Applying group-work tips and tricks to the

The IWB may resemble a play structure, a piece of chart paper, or an easel—it is up to you as a teacher to make sure students are making the most of it as an interactive tool for learning.

interactive whiteboard is not only a good idea, it is also essential when requiring small groups to independently interact on it without needing a teacher to mediate the small-group work.

The model we use is the 5 Basic Elements for cooperative group work (Johnson & Johnson, 1994). This model offers various strategies to ensure group success.

Johnsons' Five Basic Elements of Effective Group Work

1. Individual Accountability: Ensure that each individual in the group is accountable for their own learning and some part of the collaborative work.

2. Face-to-face Interaction: This requires that you set up an atmosphere for rich dialogue; i.e., small group size, proximity, and the need for face-to-face interaction.

3. Collaborative Skills: This refers to the social and collaborative skills that students need to work in small groups, such as positive commenting, listening, and acting respectfully.

4. Positive Interdependence: This requires teaching students how to interact positively with each other and other groups. This can involve a group incentive or goal.

5. Processing Academic and Social Effort: The final step in a successful group piece is a chance for the group to reflect on their experience and think critically about their involvement in the process.

For more information on the application of this theory, see Bennett & Rolheiser, 2001.

Traditional

Many teachers collaboratively create rules and routines with students, perhaps posting the rules on an anchor chart for future reference. These are usually general rules that tend to stay static the whole year.

IWB Advantage

Rules and routines are available for students at all times and in different contexts. For example, the students can see a collaboratively created list of the 5 Basic Elements as the first slide in a series outlining a small-group activity. Student groups can also be listed on slides and, if necessary, groups can be modified or changed easily. The students can touch the screen to review the elements before beginning the task. If that slide is infinitely cloned, as students complete the group work they can move the statements describing the elements they feel their group exemplified and put them next to the list of their group members, making the IWB an interactive tool for self-reflection and self-evaluation.

Once you have your small groups formed and have taught the skills necessary for successful small-group work, the interactive whiteboard lets you offer students many opportunities to practice their skills, critically think, and collaborate. You are only limited by your own creativity. You can set up the IWB to

- Link to a website that posts skills-based games. Ask students to take a screenshot of their total score for later assessment. By searching online for "interactive games," you can find many options for all subject areas.
- Use a pre-created template (see margin for a list of options) and insert the concepts, or word list, for the students to practice.
- Create your own templates for students to link to, create, and collaborate on.

Pre-created templates:
- **anagrams**
- **sorting images or text**
- **marking a world map**
- **arranging images**
- **matching images or text**
- **selecting images**
- **multiple choice**
- **arranging sentences**
- **timelines**
- **word guess**

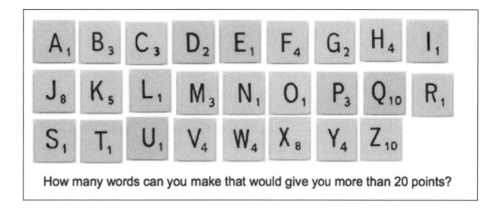

How many words can you make that would give you more than 20 points?

This screenshot models a junior-grade challenge teacher Lara Jensen created for small-group work. Using the Scrabble letters, the students collaborate to create words worth more then 20 points. Using positive interdependence, you can challenge groups to create the most unique words and score the highest number of points.

As our students navigate, find solutions, and demonstrate their knowledge, both our teaching and their learning will expand.

- Visit online resources where pre-created activities are already designed and accessible for free. There are many resources already created that can be easily accessed, downloaded, and modified if necessary.
- Post a blank screen and ask students to create the activity to match the concept.
- Use the IWB for small-group collaboration and critical thinking. Post a graphic organizer (e.g., Venn diagram, fishbone, flow chart, mind map, concept map) where students can add information, quickly and easily move their ideas, collaborate, expand or alter their ideas.
- Post a problem on the IWB, where students have an expanded repertoire of maps, images, links, and the Internet to help them solve and justify their solutions.

Connecting in the Classroom and Beyond

The interactive whiteboard allows your classroom to connect with parents and families or local businesses, and enables students to access information about the local community. Imagine students critically viewing a local news story with a teacher's guidance, going through the aisles of the local toy store and making a shopping list, sending a group e-mail home to remind parents about upcoming events, or even sharing small-group or individual work completed at school—all this is possible using the IWB to model, view, represent, and collaborate.

Virtual Field Trips

The authentic smell, feel, and look of a farm cannot be entirely replicated in the classroom. There is a charm, beyond the chaos, to a field trip. However, in our new digital world, field trips have also transformed, and you can now take your students anywhere on a virtual field trip. Virtual field trips help students feel connected to the world around them.

A virtual field trip is a multimedia experience that links a variety of digital tools, including websites, music, video, photographs, and podcast interviews. There are websites that have already created virtual field trips for you to take. You can also make your own. With a virtual field trip, you can

- Make the pace of the experience appropriate for your students.
- Focus on specific information that links to your unit of study.
- Return over and over again.

- Promote authentic inquiry by allowing students to lead you through their interests and knowledge.
- Tailor the tour to the needs of your students.

A virtual field trip is intended to complement the classroom learning, just like a real field trip. It is not intended to cover the entire unit, but rather to extend a concept or bring part of the unit to life. With a virtual field trip, you can travel anywhere. You can visit Ancient Egypt, the ocean floor, the planets, the edge of this world, and the beginnings of new worlds. The IWB is what brings a virtual field trip to life. Its sheer size and interactivity allows you to go anywhere and feel like you are there.

Traditional

Planning a field trip can be a costly and time-consuming project. Field trips require teachers to book volunteers, plan meals, supervise in a new environment, and be away from school for the whole day; this often necessitates canceling periods or other school plans. That said, it is important for students to have real-world experiences.

IWB Advantage

Make the field trip on software that incorporates sound, movies, websites, and photos. All of the multimedia included were found on free websites. See Chapter 4 for more Web 2.0 presentation tools you can use to create a virtual field trip.

At any given moment, students can visit a site, interacting with the environment by moving through photos, viewing a video, or studying an aerial map. Using a finger as a mouse, students can "look around" and even access audio tours. If a topic comes up unexpectedly, or students are discussing a recent global event, you can take them there at the touch of your finger, through maps, images, recent news reports, and online video. You can also show them the history of an event, and then freeze and drag a visual to compare it to the current event. You can create a quick timeline of events leading to the current event by dragging and sorting data. A virtual field trip brings any classroom topic to life instantly, with no additional expense and at the whim and requirements of the students.

An Interactive Idea for a Virtual Field Trip

Objective
Students will gain a better understanding of the animals, structure, and atmosphere in a rainforest.

Hook
Begin by inviting your students into the classroom with the sounds of the rainforest playing. Ask them to walk slowly and carefully, but remember to look up (because, of course, it could be raining).

Lesson
1. Post a picture of the rainforest in the IWB, with the layers apparent. Ask students to come up to drag the labels of the layers of the rainforest into the appropriate spots (they can also use the pens to circle the entire area).
2. Travel from one layer to another, from the forest floor to the emergent layer. Beginning on the forest floor, you can
- Listen carefully to the sounds and try to identify the animals that would crawl or move on the ground.
- See photos of the forest floor, using the pens to trace the plants.

- Have students drag photos of the forest floor animals into appropriate places (thinking critically of what can support the animals, where they would want to be, and what they need for camouflage).
- Link to a video on how various forest-floor animals move around and use this research to have the students move like the forest-floor animals.
- Have students jot down notes, questions, diagrams in their writing journals.
- Link the picture of the forest floor from the diagram to a new document. In that document, have students write their learning or show it in another way. This document can be a reference as students continue their journey through the rainforest.

3. Continue this experiential learning for each layer of the rainforest, possibly stopping at the canopy for a real classroom taste of durian or mango fruit.

Closure

To follow up on the rainforest virtual field trip, launch into various conversations (biodiversity, resources, advantages, destruction). Close the lesson or launch your next lesson by reflecting back on the documents created. Use the clickers to review information students learned or to survey students about what they are passionate about and their next steps.

"At first I missed writing all of the books down that Jeffrey read. It was a nice routine for us and he felt so proud of his list. But now I see the excitement when he logs into the blog. He wants to add the book he read and he wants to see what his friends are reading. I hear them talking about their comments when they play together. It made reading the book exciting, because he wants to share something from it."
—Jeff's Mom

"I want to read Project X because Nigel said they were funny on the blog."
—Jeff, age 6, who uses a class blog to track his home reading.

This screenshot shows a Grade 7 blog where the students respond to the moral of a story read in class. The students were able to read each other's ideas, respond in their own time, and comment on a peer's posting. The teacher could use this as a tracking device, or to prompt or close a discussion.

Reading Blogs

Setting up a reading blog for students is simple and supports collaboration on many levels. There are many free and easy-to-use blogs online that were designed for teaching and learning. Students can collaborate with parents or caregivers at home to read and record their thoughts on a book, and then connect to a classroom blog with separate accounts for each member of the class. Questions can be posted on the blog:

- What happened at the beginning, middle, end of the story?
- Are any characters like you? How?
- Would you recommend this book to a friend? Why?

Blog postings can be shared with the class collaboratively at school to find recommended books or to discuss stories read by members of the class. By using a blog, or public space, to share their ideas, students are thinking and writing for an authentic audience.

cathy m 5:12 pm -12-6-2010	"Don't belittle the little things." This happened at my hockey tryouts last year when the smallest kids i've ever seen our age tried out for my team. We all assumed he had no chance making our team and he would get hurt from the contact. We were wrong as he made our team and is one of the more physical players along with being a very skilled player. This is a perfect example of don't belittle little things.
benji r 5:22pm -12-6-2010	"Don't belittle the little things." I can relate to his moral becuase my older (much older) brother picks on me because im smaller than him, But then when he needs to get into tight areas, for example under his bed or behind a dresser to get his things that he dropped there, he needs me to do it, So, he asks me and I say "no. because you teased and picked on me (betlittle me). Moral: what goes around, comes around and don't belittle the little things/people.

Connecting with the Local Community

Having a sense of community and belonging is vital to our students. One of the main concepts we teach in the primary years is how students' communities operate and how they belong in their community. The interactive whiteboard can help us bring this large concept into the comfortable and safe classroom setting. They can analyze interactive maps. They can highlight or mark their favorite local places. You can empower your students by interactively looking at school information that pertains to them (e.g., school newsletters, videos of school events) and by having them work with "learning buddies," using online phone or chats on the IWB with different classes or grades to collaborate on ideas or share text they have written. Students can use programs to see how a community changes over time. You can use question prompts: *What happened before and after a natural disaster? How has the land changed over time?*

Traditional

Teachers use static images to show students the components of the community. Students might create a template of a community on big sheets of paper or a large class whiteboard. Sometimes, teachers have community representatives come into class and talk to the students about their roles or occupations. Teachers might also plan a field trip to take students out into the community to experience local places such as the grocery store, the park, or the fire station.

IWB Advantage

Using virtual field trips, online phone, and mapping programs, students can interact with people and places right on the IWB. If you use a mapping program students can use the pens to draw in buildings and services on a map or the satellite view. They can use graphics to create virtual maps of their community. You can make your class map interactive by creating a link within the file for each local icon; e.g., when the students click on the fire station, it brings them to the page they made to describe the fire station. Once you have mastered your local community, you can go on a virtual field trip to visit another community. You can zoom into other communities and look at how they are designed. You can talk online to people in communities around the world and they can share with you the similarities and differences in our lives. You can use the IWB to explore the world from your classroom.

An Interactive Idea for Looking at Community

Objective
For students to gain a sense of belonging and understanding about their local community.

Hook
- Review a definition of "community" developed in an earlier lesson.
- Together, open a fresh IWB page and brainstorm together all of the places and things that belong in a community (e.g., school, library, houses). Save these ideas on a blank file and save for easy reference.

Lesson

1. Bring up a map of the local community on the Internet. Take a screenshot of the map for centre work. Once you have the map, you can

- Find the school on the map and locate key areas that will help students gain a sense of the map.
- Have students find their homes on the map.
- Reference the file of items that belong in the community. Copy each idea separately and paste it on the map where appropriate.

2. Use the technology to zoom into the map to find specific locations. Convert the map from street view to satellite view to gain a sense of the topography of the land.

3. Use the street perspective to view the local neighborhood. Zoom out to help students gain a sense of the greater community, city, province, country, and location in the world. By playing with the map, students gain a stronger understanding of how maps work.

Closure

As a class, students virtually map out a short walking route with a highlighter, determining size of objects on the map and adding features using graphics and print. Print the map that is developed. Use the map to walk the route. Come back to reflect: *Was the route longer or shorter than expected? Did the roads bend the same way the map showed? Would students change the map? If so, how? If not, why?*

Connecting with the Global Community

By bookmarking Internet sites appropriate for young learners and creating a sharing forum, a teacher can create a depository for pictures and comments to later share with the class.

Students can visit the global community using the interactive whiteboard. They can go back in time or see events from around the world instantaneously. The global perspective allows primary students to come closer to understanding diverse cultures, environments, and people, as their personal experiences with the subjects of school curriculum are often limited. At the primary level, students are very curious about the world around them. When they ask questions, the Internet and IWB allow them to explore their questions and queries even further. For example, when young children learn about space, they want to see pictures of planets, stars, and asteroids. They like searching online for their subjects to see what pictures show up. They like to share what they find.

Once you connect your class globally, you can access many meaningful and authentic possibilities. Students can compete in live math challenges with kids at their age level from many countries. They can watch online movies and videos created by other students. They can play games created by other students from around the world, download the code, and improve on the game, reposting it to the site where others can then do the same. More and more, we are all part of an expanding digital world that is changing how we learn. There are classes, teachers, and students from all around the world that want to connect with you. Using the IWB, you can link to

- mapping around the world. By using an online mapping program, you can use the satellite view to see around the world. You can zoom in on a location and use the street view to place yourself virtually anywhere you want.
- an online video phoning system and talk to other teachers and classrooms around the world.

- penpals in countries around the world, to create projects together, to find classrooms with similar students and interests.
- social actions sites that allow students to join global activities for peace.
- Twitter to exchange ideas, feelings, and thoughts about ideas that are important in our global community.

Traditional

In traditional classrooms, we strive to provide our students with a global perspective in order to show them what life is like for people in different parts of the world. We hope that they will understand how other people, eat, play, learn, work, and interact with each other. We search out information in books or share information from our own personal adventures, as we become the bearers of information. We then create activities to relay this information to our students.

IWB Advantage

The IWB provides students with a tool to self-discover and share information. With this tool, they can become the "experts" on topics specific to their own cultures, languages, and backgrounds. Students can interact with others by virtually visiting their communities and speaking to family members and friends directly. Students can search online for graphics for visualizing unique cultural foods, tools, or art; they can bank the graphics and new vocabulary for future reference. This data can be matched to foods, tools, or other items from their own cultures. They can create documents for each culture you study and then move seamlessly though the cultures, understanding how people are similar and different around the world. Students can source out and store the information, they can compare and contrast; in the end, they can share with you their experiences, adventures, and knowledge.

An Interactive Idea for Healthy Action

Objective
Linking to your students' learning during their health classes, you can expand and connect globally on issues around healthy eating.

Hook
Refer back to the work they have completed on healthy eating, daily dietary requirements, and the four food groups. You could do this in an interactive way by using the clickers to review what the students remember from the previously studied information.

Lesson
1. Connect with the people that matter most to our students—their families. Seek out family members that live abroad and request an online phone or e-mail conversation that can be posted on the IWB.
2. Connect to other teachers online around the world—either through your own friends, or on an online site designed to connect teachers—and ask them what their students eat. Students can conduct an online survey to ask others about food around the world.

---

3. Once you have connected beyond your borders, learn together with your students. Ask and brainstorm with your students:

- What foods are common in your culture?
- What would you eat for breakfast, lunch, dinner?
- Do you snack in your culture?
- Are there any food rituals that are important to your culture?

4. With this information, students can further their research by finding photos of the food described. Drag the photos into a blank document, so they can sort and classify the foods into the four food groups. In small groups, students can create a balanced meal for family and friends abroad, using foods specific to their new friends' culture.

Closure

Bring in some of the unique or exotic foods to taste. Students can create a healthy-eating comic book at a comic creation site using their new knowledge and ideas about food and healthy eating.

4

Communicating

"How do we communicate?"
 Ms. Fleming asked her Grade 2
 students.
"Actions, speech, facial expressions,
 stories, riddles, languages, talking, e-mailing, writing, reading,
 listening, and sign language," they
 responded.

Ultimately, we strive for our students to be able to communicate in a wide variety of forms with confidence and fluency. These communication skills can be taught in many ways, from very traditional paper-and-pencil tasks to the other end of the continuum—by incorporating a range of texts to read and write. We must look critically at the literacy skills our students have and require in order to communicate effectively.

Visual text once centred around the picture in the book. It could include an artist's rendition, photos, or diagrams, and it supplemented the printed word. In the 21st century, communicating is rich with possibilities. Using the interactive whiteboard as a tool, you can create numerous learning experiences for helping readers, writers, listeners, speakers, and viewers develop new communication skills.

Literacy is more than reading stories or communicating with words. The information we read includes visual elements such as maps, diagrams, photos, tables, graphs, and moving images. These graphics work alongside movies, videos, interactive pictures, and websites. Students need support to effectively learn from these texts, even though they are exposed to these texts in and out of school all the time. Therefore, students must have the opportunity to interact with visual text in meaningful ways in the classroom. Visual texts are widely used in digital media, including the Internet, computer programs, digital games, and DVDs. Increasingly, we use visual texts to communicate complex ideas, navigate our lives, remember information, and learn content. Just as the concept of text has changed, more and more we are required to teach the skills required for visual literacy; just as we teach our students to navigate through a book, we need to show them how to apply similar skills to reading.

Teaching with Graphics

Graphics include pictures and photos in many forms. Graphics can be diagrams and symbols that support and enhance text, or pictures matched with text as illustrations. Graphics come in many forms, one of the most popular being the graphic novel, a narrative text made up of comic-like illustrations, minimal text, and speech bubbles. Using the interactive whiteboard, you can incorporate graphics into your lessons by

- Having the class collaboratively create a logo to represent their unit of study. They can continue to alter one picture until they find one that represents what they have learned. This task will require them to think critically about their learning as well as to communicate their ideas.
- Modeling how to create a comic on an online or school program. Students can create a comic collaboratively in small groups or individually. The steps

in comic-making mirror the steps in creating a story. This genre appeals to students because of the emphasis on the visual and because of the reduced text. Comics are also a powerful tool to teach the impact of words and the need to be selective when words are limited.

- Incorporating graphics into a written piece. This process involves teaching students how to find an appropriate graphic that represents what they are writing.

Teaching with Photos

Photographs have a strong appeal for students. Photos help early literacy learners link known concepts to words in poems and charts. They relay messages to readers, from facial expressions to parts of a story. They help translate concepts for English Language Learners. Photos tell stories. Photos have a powerful effect in any classroom. As teachers, we take photos of our students and post them around the room. We share photos of events and use photos to explain emotions. Using photos as visual cues is a common occurrence in classrooms. We look in a picture book, see a photo of a sad boy, and wonder aloud how he is feeling, why he is feeling that way, and how the characters might act to help him feel happy. We see a photo of an intense moment in a sporting event and we predict, analyze, and evaluate the situation based on the information in the photo. These are important discussions and the ability to get information from photos is an important skill that we explicitly and implicitly teach throughout the year.

Traditional

Cameras are well-used tools in schools. We take photos and print them on a photo-printer, or download them to a file on the computer. Photos of students can be used in the early years as a prompt to help students identify their printed names. Photos of learning activities can be shared by posting them on a bulletin board. As well, photos can also be used as visual prompts for writing.

IWB Advantage

With the interactive whiteboard, photos become an integral part of any activity. The IWB allows students to click and drag to upload their photos of people or events, and then size, manipulate, and overlay them with ease. Students can change an image by dragging a finger across it to change the size or add more color. With a photo program, students can edit photos with attention to light, sharpness, or resolution. They can expand or decrease body mass on people and take away blemishes on skin. When students learn how to manipulate a photograph, they become critical learners. It changes how they view photos in magazines or online.

In addition to manipulating photos, students can use the IWB to use the photo in interactive ways. They can hide objects or links under photos; the photos can then be revealed by a touch. Photos can be sequenced, matched with text, and saved. Students can access photos taken earlier in the year in saved files and use the slide that displays the photos for new purposes.

An Interactive Idea for Incorporating Meaningful Photos

Objective
Rethinking the concept of facial expressions, you can incorporate students' photos into a variety of lessons. This can be used to begin the year as a "getting to know you" activity, or to begin a conversation around "how we express our feelings."

Hook
Provide students with cameras and have them take photos of each other showing a variety of facial expressions: e.g., sad, happy, frustrated, surprised, worried, ecstatic.

Lesson
1. Once you have downloaded the photos, post them on a blank two-column chart template. Use simple categories, such as "positive feelings" on one side and "negative feelings" on the other. Students need to critically think about their friends' feelings in order to drag the photos to the appropriate category.
2. Clone the page of photos and change the headings to increasingly more complex categories (e.g., friendly/not friendly); students can drag and re-sort the photos many times. This activity requires the students not only to determine the facial expression and apply it to a category, but also to think of their peers and how they felt when the photo was taken.
3. Use this activity to authentically initiate a rich dialogue among the students—"Is this your sad or angry face?"—which can lead to meaningful discussions—"It is my sad face. It means that I feel left out." Audio links of the statements can be created, linked, and accessed by touching the photos on the IWB.

Closure
Save the documents and return to them during teachable moments in class. "How did Mitchell look before you spoke? What does his facial expression mean?"

You can expand on the ability to share photos and create interactive lessons for students to further explore the IWB as a visual tool. You can

- Use public websites that bank and share photographs for educational purposes.
- Post a text and have students find photos (or take photos) to complement select words: e.g., the science words, or nouns, or words that start with "s".
- Create interactive games, such as memory games, with photos of students.
- Post a map of the school in the background and use photos taken around the school for students to put in the correct place. Expand this task to photos of the neighborhood.

- Take photos of items that connect to learning units to post and teach directly; e.g., a picture of a familiar building for a unit on structures.
- Ask students to e-mail a photo from school holidays or weekends and use them as prompts for morning conversations or community circles.
- Have students each alter a copy of the same photo. Let them play with color, brightness, contrast, etc. Bring altered photos together on the IWB and discuss how changing the photo changes the mood of the image.
- Use a program to alter images. Give students time to explore ways an image can be altered. Have a class discussion about media representation. Bring up a simple image search on any topic and ask the students to identify which images might have been altered and why.

Using photos in lessons instantly connects students' lives to their learning. They feel special and important when you value their facial expressions, experiences, or perspectives. The IWB makes the process of sharing photos easy, environmentally friendly, and more efficient than printing, cutting, creating posters, and laminating.

Teaching with Movies

The large, bright screen of the interactive whiteboard creates visual appeal. It can also function as a large movie screen. You can insert a movie into the computer and display it on the interactive whiteboard. The debate for and against using movies in the classroom has lingered since the earliest technology was introduced. So much depends on the movie being shown and the message being relayed to students. Are you trying to discuss imagery, use of light and lines? Are you showing a movie to demonstrate the parts of a story: setting, characters, problem, resolution or ending? Are you showing a documentary as a visual to teach scientific knowledge: parts of the body, energy or light? The first step is to determine the purpose for showing a movie. Playing a movie on an IWB changes the possibilities for teaching. Once you have determined the purpose, you can interact with the movie before, during, and after the showing.

Previewing the Movie: Assessment for Learning

Prior to showing the movie:
1. Ask students what they expect to see in the movie.
2. Discuss why you are showing the movie and have students determine how that concept might be best demonstrated: e.g., if showing a Franklin movie or episode to talk about how friends interact, have students brainstorm how Franklin might act around his friends before watching.
3. Connect to what your students are watching at home. Explain your teaching objective and ask if they know of a video that best suits this purpose. This gives students a voice and makes meaningful connections between home and school.

During the Movie: Ongoing Assessment for Learning

Once your purpose and the movie have been selected, you can use the IWB to influence the viewing of the movie.

1. While viewing the movie, pause at the exact moment you want to highlight. IWB tools can help you draw attention to the teaching moments:

- Take a screenshot and use it as a reference in later lessons.
- Use the pens to shine a spotlight on a visual effect you want to stress.
- Use the pens to zoom in on a part of the movie that you want to highlight.

2. Once you have paused or highlighted the portion of the movie you want to interact with, add layers to the lesson by

- Writing on the screen: circle the main characters, identify the setting, search for clues that might foreshadow upcoming scenes.
- Pausing on the main character: use the pens to do a character analysis directly on the character.
- Turning off the sound and allowing students the opportunity to create their own dialogue, to use visual clues to predict and interact with the characters. Students can explain what is happening and what might happen, and they can fill in the voices of the characters.
- Pausing on a setting shot: use the clues in the picture to guess where the movie could have been filmed (looking at landscape, climate, vegetation).

This snapshot is from a lesson on complex words with a silent e (from LeapFrog's *Word Caper* DVD). Students reviewed the effect of the "magic e" and then brainstormed and used the pens to add consonant–vowel–consonant words to the beginning to make complex "magic e" words.

© 2004 LeapFrog Enterprises, Inc. *Word Caper* was previously released as *Talking Words Factory 2: Code Word Caper.*

After the Movie: Discussions and Assessment of Learning

When you have completed watching the movie, you can once more use the IWB as an assessment tool:

- Use the screenshot as a diagram. At a learning centre, have students label the concepts you were using the movie to demonstrate.
- Take a series of screenshots from the movie and have students drag and sort the shots in order.
- Create a chart with labels for Setting, Characters, Problem, Solution, and Ending. Have students drag the screenshots into the appropriate spot on the chart.

- Use a screenshot from the movie as a backdrop for practicing basic skills.
- Have students look back at their brainstorming ideas from prior to watching the movie and sort the ideas into two categories: "It happened in the movie" and "It didn't happen in the movie."
- Students can use the ideas that were not used in the movie to create their own endings.

Traditional

Teachers take the opportunity to show movies to students as the movies relate to the theme or learning goal in the classroom. Often students are asked to predict before or during the movie, and respond to prompts afterward. Watching a movie can be a passive experience, or students can actively get engaged by completing a task (e.g., recording ideas on sticky notes) as they watch.

IWB Advantage

With the IWB, movies become an interactive learning lesson. The movie is not the main focus, but is rather a tool to teach a concept. Students can touch the screen to pause the movie at moments they think are key so they can start a class discussion about their ideas; or to pause the movie when they find something worth sharing to take a quick screenshot to interact with later. You can take screenshots of various parts of the movie and transfer them to a blank slide so that students can sequence the movie after the viewing. The screenshots can also be used as visual prompts for writing. The movie can be darkened, lightened, or highlighted using the pens and other tools to draw students' attention to specific elements of moviemaking or content. It is easy to compare other graphics to movie graphics by showing other slides side-by-side with the movie. As students become involved in the process, they watch the movie with a critical eye and search for relevant information independently for sharing as a whole class.

See Chapter 6 for more on assessment for learning.

An Interactive Idea for Using Movies

Objective
The movie selection *Ferngully: The Last Rainforest* connects with the theme of empathy. Use students' prior knowledge about fairy tales to help uncover the message of empathy.

Hook: Preview and Assessment for Learning
- Prior to showing the movie, show the trailer. Pause the preview at various stages (beginning, middle, and end). Talk about the use of lighting (dark to start and then brighter at the end). Connect this to a talk about the structure of fairytales (Ask: *How does the preview match the structure of a fairytale?*). Bring up a saved file on the structure of a fairytale for a quick reference and have the students use the pens to directly write on the file with clues from the movie.
- An alternative is to find a picture of the video cover and put it on the IWB to preview. Have students use the pens to identify the elements of a story (i.e. characters, setting). Ask: *What do you think the message of the movie might be? What feelings do you think you might have during this movie?* Have them draw or write down what they think the movie will be about.

Lesson: During the Movie and Assessment for Learning

1. Pause the movie once Zak and Crysta have been introduced. Take a screen shot of Zak and one of Crysta. Create a Venn diagram on a blank page and compare the personalities of the characters. Ask: *What are some of the problems with Zak's attitude?* Post some difficult words, such as "respectful" or "sympathetic," and have students drag the words to the appropriate place.

2. Pause the movie at the point where Zak first shows empathy. Separate students into small groups and have them enact what might happen in the rest of the movie. You might give them small hints for their dramatic pieces, such as *happy ending, unhappy ending,* or *cliff-hanger.*

3. Continue to take screenshots of Zak as his character develops. *Why did Zak's attitude change? What is Crysta's role in changing Zak's attitude?* Refer back to your Venn diagram character analysis and use a different color pen to add more detail that shows character development.

Closure: Discussion and Assessment of Learning

- Ask students why they think you showed this movie, connecting it to the discussion or unit of study. What is the main message of this movie? What part of the movie best represented empathy? When did Zak first display signs of empathy?

- Using the IWB, take screenshots of the movie and have students sort the photos into the correct order. In a learning centre, allow each student to find a point in the movie that demonstrates empathy. Have them take screenshots of this moment and save it on a file. Come together and have students sort the empathy photos on a continuum, with one end being *Beginning to show empathy* and the other end being *Taking action with empathy.*

- Have students "think, pair, share" their opinions on the message of the movie. Once the pair has determined a message, they can write it on the IWB, making changes and erasing when necessary. Save these messages to use in other units, to compare with other stories, or to access as a discussion point when, for example, empathy was not shown on the playground.

- Have students connect this learning to their own lives: *How can we show empathy?* Make a list of their ideas on a spreadsheet and convert it into a graph to mark each time they complete an empathic action. Save this file on the desktop so that students can easily access it and take ownership in updating their actions.

Think–pair–share is a simple strategy in which students are asked to think about a concept or question on their own, then collaboratively discuss it with a partner; finally, some students are chosen to share ideas with the larger group. This strategy gives all students an opportunity to share, either with a partner or the whole class. It also increases accountability for all students.

Teaching with Online Videos

Why would we use online videos? There are moments when, as much as we try to describe concepts for students, a picture really is worth a thousand words, and a quick visual is the best tool to demonstrate the concept. Explaining how the rotation and tilt of the earth causes seasons is a wonderful flashlight-and-globe lesson; following it up with a quick online video that shows the earth's movement helps further solidify the concept for our students. Another example involves story writing, as the IWB can be a strong visual tool to reinforce the message of how to understand stories by manipulating a short video and connecting it to concepts being taught. Many young students love building; they understand construction. Before beginning a unit on storytelling and fairy tales, students need to be able to identify the key elements of a story (setting, characters, problem, climax, resolution, and ending). This can be modeled by deconstructing a story. By showing a two-minute construction video, you can refresh the concept of "construction." With the IWB, you are able to rewind the video, showing "deconstruction" while writing on the screen and pointing out the careful undoing (rather than destroying). Play the video with and without sound. Students can fill in the text orally when the volume is turned off.

Online videos, as well as any video-sharing websites, are useful tools for teachers. They allow us to bring our students closer to difficult concepts. We can use all of the advantages of the IWB that we would with a regular movie to highlight and share information. These sites also open the door to serious conversations, such as what it means to leave a digital footprint and the benefits and drawbacks of sharing a video online. Teaching "netiquette"—as students communicate with others through social media, sharing sites, and publishing—helps educate and protect students from negative consequences. Asking critical questions, such as "Would you post a video on line? What would you feel comfortable posting, and why?," helps open the door to dialogue and creates an understanding of what is appropriate and what is not appropriate.

There are now various Web 2.0 tools you can use to enhance your sharing of online movies or other public videos. We can begin our search on sites created for previewing videos. Some websites (e.g., Kideos.com and SchoolWaxTV.com) preview and bank videos so that students can search on these sites and you can feel confident that the videos they are searching are age-appropriate. Some sites (e.g., TubeChop.com) allow you to isolate sections of public videos for students to view independently. These sites enable you to share a section of a video while eliminating inappropriate or irrelevant information. When you alter and prepare public videos, you can use video selections for students' independent work or centre rotations.

Other Web 2.0 tools allow commenting possibilities on public videos. Sites such as www.blip-snips.com allow students to make comments directly on the video, so they can share their opinions and ideas on a video directly on the text within a secure site.

Netiquette

Online videos have altered the way we interact with videos. As digital natives, students lack any sense of hesitation and their products require much less polishing than we show when interacting with recording and publishing digital media. As educators, we walk the fine line between wanting to share everything our students need to interact with this quickly developing technological world and concern about its appropriateness and its instant connection. So, what is our role? We must begin with previewing each piece of text to ensure that the content matches our expectations. Digital text should

- Connect to the message we are sending.
- Offer visual and graphic representations that enhance learning.
- Be clear of inappropriate messages that we do not intend to discuss with our students.

Web 2.0 tools, such as www.viewpure.com, allow you to share a video without ads or comments.

Traditional

We teach our students about safety on roads, how to deal with strangers, and how to interact safely with each other. While the digital world brings many exciting and important possibilities for education and social interaction, the world that our students live in requires that we also teach them about interacting safely with technology.

IWB Advantage

Netiquette and how to interact safely with technology needs to be taught *using* technology. The IWB is the ideal space to interact with, teach, model, and share safe technology practices. You can post blogs or Tweets by unknown people and try to create an image of them based on their comments. Using different colored pens to highlight positive and negative comments, and a separate color for questionable comments, students can critically look at language and how we interpret information. You can display the history of comments and use search engines to show the impact comments have made on other people. Students can create comments, then drag and rank them according to the impact they would have on different people (e.g., friends, teachers, parents, strangers). The IWB provides students with a safe place to learn about what is appropriate when using technology.

Resources to Help Understand the Concepts
http://www.unicel.com/standup/pdf/StandUpGuide.pdf
http://www.stopcyberbullying.org/

See page 78 for more on concept attainment.

An Interactive Idea for Looking at Cyberbullying

Objective

Defining cyberbullying and comparing it to traditional bullying; revealing the laws around cyberbullying; providing students with appropriate responses to cyberbullying.

Hook

Begin with a concept-attainment activity. Collaboratively sort examples of traditional bullying on one side and cyberbullying on the other without labeling the lists. Let students determine the label for each list.

COLUMN 1	COLUMN 2
When someone says something unkind Face-to-face Can be a physical attack	When someone types something unkind online Bully assumes that the negative behavior is anonymous

Ask students:

- Which side would you add "happens in e-mails, blogs, Tweets"? Move the statement where you think it should go.
- Which side would you add "creates a victim"? Move the statement where you think it should go. If you disagree, change the position of the statement.
- What can you add? Which side can it go on?
- Can anyone guess the title of either column?

Brainstormed titles can be listed at the top of the columns and, when consensus is reached, the discarded titles can be easily erased or dragged into the criteria section.

Lesson

1. Define cyberbullying. Begin with what students have added to the column and what words they use to define this concept. You may want to add any of the following:

- Direct Cyberbulling: when the bully directly confronts the victim (on a chat site, blog, texting, etc.)
- Cyberbullying by Proxy: when the bully gets someone else to attack the victim.

Use the clickers to take an anonymous survey about students' experiences with cyberbullying.

2. In small groups, students create a profile for a cyberbully. Ask: *Why might the bully be acting this way* (e.g., jealousy, seeking revenge, low self esteem, bully wants to feel powerful). Post the profiles on the IWB and look for common statements in the various profiles by circling key words using the IWB pens in different colors.

3. Ask: *What is the outcome? What can ultimately happen?*
- To further the conversation, find a quick clip by accessing an online movie about cyberbullying or creating a touch-and-reveal template on the IWB.
- Cyberbullies can be punished by parents, school authorities, friends, teachers, law enforcers. Quickly search your location and local laws about cyberbullying to ensure you are providing your students with accurate and up-to-date information.

4. Task: Have students work in groups to create a digital presentation or flow chart to show how a typical teenager could/should respond to cyberbullying in a positive manner; e.g., gathering evidence with screenshots, talking with others and adults.

Closure
Present the presentations and flowcharts, using the IWB. Discuss the various responses.

Teaching with Websites/Pages

When teaching with websites, begin with what you already know. How do you teach a picture book or a novel? Do you start with a preview: show the front and back cover, read the summary aloud, skim the pages together? Do you carefully introduce the book, referring to the visuals, decoding difficult words together, referring to the elements of the story (setting, characters)? Do you stop at key moments, recall it together, and then foreshadow the next moment? Do you end the book study with a summary, gathering opinions, sharing alternate endings? You already know how to introduce text to students. You just need to transfer these skills to the graphic visuals in today's digital texts.

When selecting a website, begin with a preview. Put yourself in the shoes of a student and visit the site your students will be visiting. Once you have navigated through the various tabs and menu options and feel confident, model this process for students. The IWB is the ideal tool to showcase a website for students. You can directly model your expectations, step by step, and they can follow along. You can anticipate that students might need to see instructions again by recording your steps on the IWB. Rather than repeating the steps again, just hit Play and your steps will be displayed again.

Once you have determined and previewed the site that will best suit your students, the opportunity for teaching begins. You know that your students are on websites at home. You know they can navigate to meet some of their needs. But, just as you teach students solid reading strategies to help them digest, comprehend, and evaluate books, you also need to give them strategies to understand websites and web pages. Teaching using integrated texts, such as web pages and websites, means that teachers must consider many different aspects of literacy learning.

For some types of websites and Web 2.0 tools, see Chapter 5.

Using the Four Resources Model

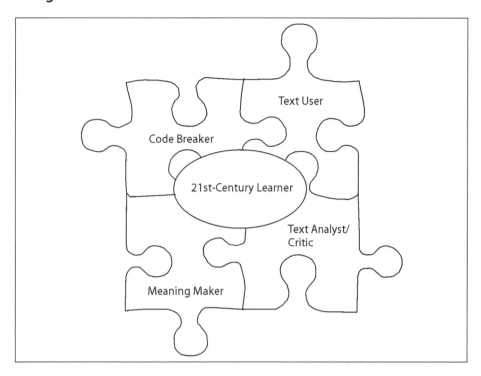

To help guide this section, we use this framework (from Luke & Freebody, 1999). We find this model comprehensive and inclusive of the critical components of how to read media for interactive learning. The model defines the four roles of a literate learner as code breaker, meaning maker, text user, and text analyzer. Teachers can address each role in a balanced way with all the other roles.

It is the complex interaction of the four roles that supports literacy learning. Literacy learning involves more than a single skill, and is an interaction of skills and resources that the literate learner draws upon to make meaning from texts of many types. Just as we would teach a text in a book thoroughly, we must explicitly teach digital media in order for students to effectively deal with digital literacy learning.

As students communicate using digital technology, they read, write, and use a wide variety of texts. They view videos and graphics, preview web pages, and play on websites. They think about the texts in their lives, how they will use them, their purposes and their messages. It is our role as educators to make sure that the definition of communication is one that will help prepare our students for the challenges they will encounter in the wide world that stands before them.

Breaking the Code

The role of code breaker is important: students are taught to recognize and use the features and structures of texts, including breaking down words, sentence structure, text organization, graphics, and other visuals to break the "code" of text. This can be as basic as using phonics to teach letter–sound correspondence when reading. It can be as complex as interpreting a web page and decoding the words, organization, and images to determine the meaning. Using the IWB, you can model, teach, and have your students

- Identify the parts of the web page in an interactive manner. Highlight the address and show how it often connects to the title (e.g., the title for the URL www.kidsclick.org is *KidsClick*). The title is also known as the site ID and often answers the question "What site is this?"
- Take screenshots of a few popular websites and identify the parts that are similar or different (consider using a graphic organizer).
- Navigate through various linking pages. Often a website has layers of navigation, with a menu that links to the various pages in the site. Highlight the top tabs that link to other pages and shine a spotlight on the side menu bar that links to sections on the page you are currently on.
- Find the page name and identify where you are on the website using the menu bar.
- Use the pens to identify the footer at the bottom of the page and talk about why it exists.
- Create a fishbone graphic organizer to lay out the various parts of the website, placing the main topic at the head and following with the subtopics. The subtopics are then supported by details.
- Debug the web page: take a screenshot and use it to record the steps in understanding the web page and navigating through the various links. Play back this lesson at a learning centre to model for the students.

This screenshot shows the parts of a typical web page labeled. In this lesson, the teacher and students *debugged* the text genre of the web page.

Making Meaning

Taking the role of meaning maker empowers students to use prior knowledge and experience to construct and communicate meaning when reading, writing, and speaking. Using the IWB, our students can
- Predict what visuals would complement the website they will be visiting.
- Predict what advertisements would support the visiting website.

- Interpret the dominant visuals on the website. Is it marketing or was it created by the website design to support the message of the web page? How do we know?
- Read short bits of text and infer meaning from them.
- Answer literal comprehension questions about the text; for example, "How many eyes do spiders have?"

Using Texts

Teaching students to be text users supports their understanding that the purpose and audience help to determine the way a text is structured. Elements such as the formality, sequence of components, and placement of graphics or text are important, and this knowledge helps students read and write text pragmatically, applying their knowledge in the real world of reading the web. Using the IWB as both a visual and interactive tool, you can demonstrate how to navigate the Internet:

- Bring students to a fake website. Ask critical questions: *What can we learn from this website? Do we have any questions about this topic? How can we verify if this website is legitimate?*
- Complete a search together on a topic. Model the various tools: web, images, video, news, books, and maps. Have students determine what exactly they are looking for and decide together which type of information will best answer the question (e.g. Are all bulldozers yellow? This can be answered using the images).
- Refer back to the web address (URL) on the webpage. Complete a search and teach students to navigate using web addresses and synopses to select the best website.
- Create a blank research page and have the students fill it in with facts that they have learned while surfing the Internet.
- Provide students with a piece of paper and pencil crayons. Have them research a topic using images. Ask them to draw an accurate diagram or picture using the information from the other visuals.

Traditional

Teachers often have students do research using nonfiction texts found in the school library or classroom. They help students do research online, bookmarking websites that are appropriate for research or pairing up students to read websites together. Introducing websites or the digital text genre of web pages is often done by projecting a web page on a screen and pointing out different features, reading parts of the text out to students, or doing shared readings of the text, and having them consider the validity of certain statements on the web, perhaps jotting down valid/invalid statements in a notebook.

IWB Advantage

Using the interactivity of the IWB, students and teachers can write directly on web pages to highlight features of the text. Text can be retyped using the keyboard function and moved to a blank notebook page to be further examined. Teachers can take screenshots of advertisements or questionable content and copy it to other blank notebook pages, creating a library of information that students need

Fake websites are are created for the purpose of educating students about thinking critically; e.g., saving the tree octopus from extinction (http://zapatopi.net/treeoctopus/) or buy dehydrated water (www.buydehydratedwater.com).

to be cautious about. Students can revisit pages created within this lesson when using web pages in the future, to discuss and activate prior knowledge about the genre. As students gain confidence and awareness about how to navigate digital text, they can bank their favourite web pages or pages that might be useful to peers by simply clicking on the screen to bookmark the page.

An Interactive Idea for Text Using

In 2005, Yahoo indexed 18.2 billion websites. Searching for the information your students want can be a daunting task.

Objective
You can teach your students how to use search engines and to think critically when searching for information.

Hook
Using the IWB as a model, perform a search for a common topic using a common search engine. Show students that, as they begin to type the word, a variety of options are presented. If they cannot find their topic, they might have misspelled the word (spelling does have a purpose). Walk them through the text features of a web page, highlighting various tabs that change the format of information (i.e., Web, Images, Movie, Map, Research). Use the IWB pens or Highlight option to have students interact with the text by circling or underlining different text features. Model how to read the summaries of the websites and the URL address to determine if the site is worth visiting. Model multiple times how to use images, videos, and various web addresses. Copy parts of the information and paste it on another slide or blank document to highlight questionable information found on websites.

Lesson
Assign your students the task of answering a question using a search engine. Would text, an image, or a movie answer their question best? What should be entered as the topic to best find the answer?

Closure
Once students gain comfort searching for information, they can record a question that they are wondering about and find the answer. Using the IWB, you can store the questions and answers for later activities. This newly found information can be digitally shared as a class or in their portfolios.

Analyzing Text and Critical Use

The role of text analyzer is one through which students are taught that texts are not neutral, that they represent different points of view and perspectives, and that other views and perspectives may be missing. Together, you and your students can

- Analyze the background images, font, and color. Complement this study with their prior knowledge from art. How does the color, font, and imagery make the website appealing?
- Compare various sites that have the same message and rank them based on different criteria (e.g., user-friendly, easy-to-read, use of graphics). Use the screenshot option so that students can mark up the sites.
- Research a site and find out who created it. Why was this website created?

The importance of the role of text analyzer becomes clear when you consider that companies use websites for marketing purposes. The visual display on a website is powerful. Websites are organized, color-coordinated, filled with images, and they often contain marketing. How do you teach students to navigate freely while trying to shelter them from inappropriate visuals? Just as you would preview a book prior to reading it, preview the web pages you assign to students. Ensure that the content, vocabulary level, and navigation are age-appropriate. Are there advertisements? Do the ads flip or rotate? Is there a chance that students will be exposed to a visual you did not intend them to see? Incorporating your critical-thinking skills, ask students:

- What are advertisements?
- Why do you think they exist?
- What do you think they are trying to do?
- What companies would market on a kids' site?
- On which sites do you think a toystore should advertise?
- How do the creators of websites make an ad appeal to a young child, a pre-teen, a teenager?

Empower your students to feel "smarter than marketing" by challenging them to look critically at ads. Just as students are exposed to commercials at home, they will be exposed to marketing online. This opens an opportunity for you to address digital text in a meaningful and critical manner. It forces students to think, while it educates them about the structure of the text that fills their lives. Students will be exposed to advertising and other unwanted visuals while navigating websites. Addressing the issues in an honest and upfront manner allows you to engage in a dialogue with your students and create the platform for understanding text.

5 Creating

As students are given the opportunity for creativity, they will become increasingly engaged. We know that motivation increases as students' efforts are valued and as students are given the autonomy to make choices within a range of options. Tasks and activities can be determined with input from students and based on students' questions about the content they are studying. The IWB gives the teacher the opportunity to record, revisit, and use students' ideas to present different activities. It can also be used as a tool that supports a range of choices and allows students to try ideas, make mistakes (and easily fix them), show their friends and teachers their progress, and receive feedback while working as individuals or in groups toward an authentic product.

Consider this quote from Paul Lockhart's "A Mathematician's Lament."

> Children can write poems and stories as they learn to read and write. A piece of writing by a six-year-old is a wonderful thing, and the spelling and punctuation errors don't make it less so. Even very young children can invent songs, and they haven't a clue what key it is in or what type of meter they are using.

The same is true of digital technology. Students do not need to know every detail of a digital tool in order to use it and create with it. One of the characteristics of 21st-century learners is their ability to be creative in our ever-changing world—to find new and exciting solutions to both simple and complex problems. Young children are inundated with information from many sources, both at home and at school. As they integrate that information to form and share knowledge, creativity and innovation are crucial. There are many opportunities for young learners to display creativity using the IWB. From sharing their learning by contributing to a class presentation, to creating a digital product on the IWB using Web 2.0 tools, each child will look at problems differently and must have the opportunity to find solutions that allow for critical and creative thinking and focus on plausible ideas instead of correct answers. On the large display of the IWB, students can display creations in full screen or combine a visual display, sound, and movement. Creating on the IWB opens up endless possibilities.

Starting the Creative Process

See Chapter 6 for more on assessment for learning.

A natural first step is to find out what the students know. Brainstorming for their prior knowledge is a common technique to assess for learning. The objective of a brainstorming session is to access as much prior knowledge—including ideas and questions—about a topic as possible. While students share prior knowledge, more ideas and questions naturally occur. To gather students' ideas and questions, you can use the IWB in various ways:

- Create a blank template or web organizer and write students' ideas and/or questions as they start talking about their new unit. The sticky note application will let students move, classify, sort, add, and delete ideas, as each idea is in its own contained area.

- Post a brainstorm chart as a background. This allows you to interact with your students in an activity, prompting them to add more ideas as they occur. If help is available, have someone write or type the questions or ideas for younger students. This allows them to ask bigger questions without worrying about trying to get down their ideas.

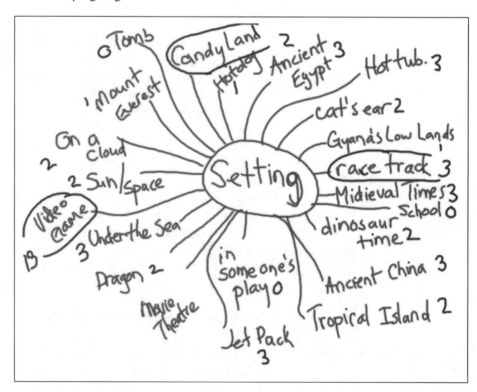

- Find a clip from an online video, a graphic, or a movie trailer that sets the tone for the upcoming unit and use it to prompt dialogue.

- Do a quick online image search on the topic for images that activate prior knowledge. Drag them into the background, where students can write the facts they already know directly over the images.
- Save the brainstorm file and reopen it another day. The interactive and manipulative nature of the IWB allows you to quickly drag, expand, or add new ideas.
- Create a large graffiti wall on the IWB, or use a Web 2.0 graffiti wall application. A graffiti wall is simply a blank space where students can freely add single words or sentences and share pictures, ideas, or quotes to represent their ideas. Using digital technology, they can also record their voices to post ideas on the graffiti wall.

Using as many traditional and digital tools as possible to "frontload" your students helps them gain an understanding of what they already know and what they would like to learn more about. This process creates a richer unit as you tailor your instruction to what students are motivated to learn about. For a unit on plants, bringing in plants, sourcing thematic books to use throughout the unit, displaying tools that are used for planting, posting a world map outlining vegetation, and showing a short video about how plants grow helps our students ask meaningful questions. Such questions can refer to specific terminology (What is chloroplast?), draw attention to objects (What does fruit have to do with plants?), or make personal connections (Why does my uncle use that in his garden?). The more we understand what our students already know and want to know, the more we can facilitate meaningful and authentic learning.

One strategy that helps create a classroom where students feel safe to take risks is to encourage them to ask questions but not take ownership for them. At first this might seem odd. Think of it this way: if a student has a question and can write it on the IWB without attaching a name, the student does not have to worry that he or she is asking a "stupid question." The student feels safe, because any question is accepted and anyone can answer it. Your classroom can become a collective where ideas are posted, moved, answered, or combined. Students can write a question on a digital sticky note and post it on the IWB, bringing that question to life. Sticky notes can be easily manipulated, dragged, altered. When the class as a whole is responsible for the list of questions, students feel free to move the questions around, make links, combine questions, and delete ones that do not relate or are easy to answer, making room for more. The class can gain a better perspective on the unit and take a sense of collective ownership.

Organizing Ideas: Using Graphic Organizers

Once we have gathered our ideas and questions, using the interactive whiteboard as a tool for brainstorming naturally leads to organizing ideas. Organizing ideas is one of the most powerful ways to make sense of information. Graphic organizers are visual frameworks that support learning by organizing, clarifying, and connecting ideas. They can also be used to assess or evaluate learning. Organizers can contain graphics, words, voices, and other elements. The IWB is the ideal tool for interacting with graphic organizers. It enables students to drag ideas and sort them. Using the IWB to create graphic organizers provides an interactive and engaging environment in which students can critically think and justify their decisions. The IWB allows students to revisit the organizers over time. They can represent their ideas through a number of modes by dragging graphics or words from other Internet sites into the graphic organizers that are in progress.

There are many ways to organize ideas using the IWB:

See Bennett & Rolheiser (2001), for more information on deBono's Six Thinking Hats and Concept Attainment.

- Create a template for Edward deBono's Six Thinking Hats: each hat represents a category of complex thinking, such as feelings, information, caution, meta-cognition, offering suggestions, or looking for the positive. Using the IWB, students critically sort their ideas and questions into each perspective by dragging, debating, and dragging again. This exercise will help identify which perspectives students might be missing.

- Use the IWB for concept attainment. In this instructional strategy, the teacher provides "yes" and "no" examples and then has students develop the categories based on commonalities between the examples. Students compare like examples and contrast them with unlike examples. It allows students to think about a concept and develop their own knowledge of it, rather than being told what a concept is. Using the IWB, various sources for building background knowledge and activating schema can be found online and shared. Videos can be paused and the IWB pens can be used to write over images in videos or books. Concept attainment is more powerful on the IWB, as examples can be moved to different categories as students puzzle out possibilities.

- Create a two-column T-chart for students to use when comparing and contrasting ideas; the ideas can easily be dragged between columns.

- Have students sort ideas and questions into a four-column organizer, which can be labeled by students and teacher: *Questions I have/What I think I know/Wonderings/New learning*.

Prior to this screenshot, the students played with rocks and minerals and asked questions aloud. Questions were recorded on the IWB by the teacher. In this lesson, they sorted their questions into four groups, based on which questions they thought were similar. They also created a category for each group of questions. This guided the learning, as students came back to delete answered questions and move questions into new categories as they gained more knowledge.

Week 1 Made

How did a rock become a rock?

Where do different rocks come from?

Is sand just tiny rocks?

How come rocks have holes in them?

What are rocks made of?

Do rocks come from mountains?

How are they formed?

Week 2 Old

How do rocks get stuff in it?

How old is the oldest rock?

Why are most rocks dirty?

What are there only a few multi rocks?

Where does that come from (fossil)?

Why are rocks old?   How are fossils made?

Week 3 Crystals

How long did crystals take to form? How can you tell?

Why does this one have lots of holes?

Why are crystals outside, but not inside?

Is there diamonds in rocks?

Why are crystals shiny?

Why do some have crystals?

?

What kinds of rock are in people's houses?

Week 4 Look like

Why does the rock have shiny stuff on it?

Why are some rocks hard and some rocks are fragile?

How can some rocks write?

Why are some rocks so smooth?

Why are some rocks smooth and some are not?

Why is my rock yellow?   Why do some rocks have giant cracks and some don't?

Why does it look like plastic? Fake?   Why are some bumpy and some smooth?

Why are there colours in rocks? How?

Why is this shiny? What makes it silver?

- Have students create a word web. They can add or take out words, reorganizing the web as they make new connections and rethink previous ideas

In this screenshot, students collaboratively added, deleted, and connected the new science vocabulary they learned throughout their unit on the sun. Prior to a lesson, they would refer back to what they knew; after the lesson, they would add information about new concepts and think about what previous ideas it connected to.

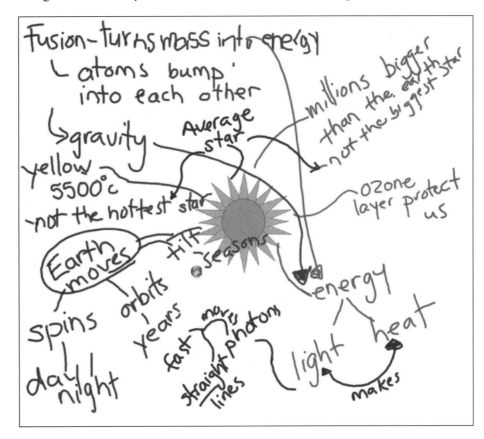

Learning theory tells us that students are more likely to learn if they are able to organize their thinking into conceptual frameworks. That is why tables, charts, graphs, and organizers are common ways to present information—they support understanding. Similarly, as students conceptualize information as knowledge, organizing the information for our learners is a strategy that supports learning, thinking, and creativity. Using the IWB to work with graphic organizers at the beginning, middle, and end of a unit of study helps students build on information. When you use a graphic organizer at the beginning of a topic and continue to access it while students acquire a richer understanding, they evaluate their new-found knowledge and sort it into the categories they have created. By saving the graphic organizer, you can continually pull it up to add new ideas. As the unit progresses, students can reconceptualize their organization of ideas, and add or alter the graphic to share the growing information. At the end of the unit, this graphic organizer displays students' full and complex understanding of the topic.

Traditional

There are many ways teachers access prior knowledge, wonderings, and learning. A KWL chart (*What do I Know/What do I Want to Know/What have I Learned*) organizer or any type of recording chart is typically used prior to reading nonfiction to activate prior knowledge, to question, and then to record new information. Students brainstorm and record ideas on chart paper, with pairs of students working together to complete the organizer or students working independently. The information that is recorded on paper is hard to change or move as new information is gained. Even recording on a standard whiteboard is complicated, as information changes and moves throughout the research process.

IWB Advantage

Using the IWB, teachers can record information from the whole class. Organizers can be set up for pairs or groups of students on subsequent blank documents in a file. Students can record information as of a given date, and then update that information as the research process continues; they can drag, add, copy from files, and delete unwanted information collaboratively. Using the IWB, the learning process is living and breathing. Students circulate between what they know, what they wonder, and what they learn. It is not a linear process, but learning that continues to evolve and grow with the students.

Using Tony Stead's RAN organizer on the IWB makes knowledge sharing, thinking, and wondering more accessible to students as they read nonfiction texts, research, and gather information. See *Reality Checks* (Stead, 2006) for more on this strategy.

An Interactive Idea for Reading and Analyzing Nonfiction

Objective
To help students ask questions, answer them, and track their own learning.

Hook
Use one of the frontloading activities from pages 76–77 to engage the students in a new topic of study.

Lesson
1. Post a chart on the IWB. Use categories that reflect prior knowledge and new information gained from research (Stead, 2006).

What I think I know	Confirmed (Yes! I was right!)	Misconceptions	New information	Wonderings
• students record prior knowledge they have about a topic	• students research to confirm prior knowledge	• students research to discard prior knowledge	• students research to find additional information not stated in prior knowledge	• students raise questions based on the new information gathered

Column 1: This allows the reader to acknowledge that all background knowledge may not be accurate.
Column 2: When reading confirms that background knowledge is correct, the student's statement moves from the first column to this column.
Column 3: When reading does not confirm what the student thought was correct, the statement moves to this column.
Column 4: Through the use of nonfiction text, either digital or print, students gain new information and record their findings here.
Column 5: A place for children to raise questions during and after reading.
2. Have students post their ideas on interactive sticky notes in the first column. Save this chart on the desktop so that students can access it as they learn more.
3. To maintain interest, open the chart and see if any of the sticky notes can move. Have you learned anything that connects to one of your previous ideas? For example, have you found new information about what you think you know? Was it a misconception or was it factual information?

Connecting to Create: Incorporating Other Digital Tools

The interactive whiteboard is a wonderful blank slate. It can be used on its own to share information, model, and create presentations. There are other digital tools that can be incorporated to create more possibilities. With these digital tools and the IWB, you open more possibilities for creating, exploring, and sharing information. When you combine the digital tools that you have, such as cameras and microphones, multiple options are presented. As our technology develops, more tools are created to complement the interactive whiteboard.

Creating with Digital Cameras

See Chapter 4 for ideas on incorporating photos into lessons.

Digital photography has changed the way we take photos. Digital natives ask, "Can I see my picture?" immediately after taking the photo, and are able to evaluate the photo and determine if it needs to be retaken. We can take multiple photos without concerns about cost, printing, and developing. We can take mediocre photos or photos in less than ideal settings, and we can alter them on the computer, playing with light and color, and even changing the background. We can incorporate critical aspects in our teaching by asking: *Why are photos altered? Who alters them? What would be the effect of altering different photos, such as a home for sale or a model in a magazine?*

Traditional

Why do we take photos? In many ways, they are a record of what has been done. They are displayed or shared. Typically this involves posting them on a bulletin board or e-mailing them to a parent. They might be printed for a portfolio piece.

IWB Advantage

Using the IWB, you can begin to display and share photos in an interactive way. With a click, students can access stocks of photos. With easy access to photos, students no longer need to use them as a final record, but also to support ongoing learning. They can use the photos to support a piece they are writing or to refer to an event. They can drag the photos into documents to support ideas they have. You can create a new file and keep a permanent yet always changing store of photos. Students can take a free moment to add text, speech bubbles, or backgrounds to the photos.

Making Movies

Movie making is an engaging process for students of any age. It allows students to correct mistakes, rerecord, and create a polished presentation. There are a variety of free tools and programs online. Movies can be made with a camera (connecting a group of still shots), video camera, or other supplies, such as artwork or clay for animation. Movies can involve voice-overs (recording speech while the action is taking place), transitions (moving between scenes easily), and effects that can make a student project look very professional.

Just as they would prepare for any storytelling activity, students can use planning strategies to think about their movie long before the actual recording begins. They can use a graphic organizer to work through their main message, plot, and characters. On the IWB, they can touch and drag their ideas from one spot to another, editing and developing their movie plans.

Here is an outline for making a movie as a class project:

1. Brainstorm a topic or idea.
2. Assessment: Think about the end. How will the project be assessed? Create a class rubric or discuss the learning goals and success criteria for the task.
3. Storyboarding: Create the scenes that will be in the movie. Using the IWB, students can move visuals from one scene to the next, adding and deleting ideas easily until the plan is complete.
4. Scriptwriting: The class can write the script, breaking the project into scenes, or groups can work through it as a whole.
5. Consensus: Post the script on the IWB so students can read it aloud, in character. Work through and make edits directly on the IWB to polish the script. Students understand that the piece is always changing and can be easily altered.

6. Design: Gather the necessary costumes, props, supplies, and materials to make the script come to life.

7. Dramatize: Rehearse until ready to shoot.

8. Shoot: Record the movie. Take several recordings so that students can choose the best scenes when they edit.

9. Edit: Use the IWB to edit the movie collaboratively. Choose the best takes and put them together narratively. Add music, voice-overs, and transitions.

10. Share: Post the movie on the class website or blog, or make a DVD copy for each student to take home.

Making movies is always appealing to students as a form of creating. Students can make movies for a variety of purposes:

- Creating a slide show with a series of photos and voice-overs to tell a story.
- Teaching a math, geography, history concept to others.

In this screenshot, one of teacher Kathryn O'Brien's Grade 5 students created a movie to explain a math concept. The students took a photo of the steps taken to solve the math problem, downloaded the photos into a movie program, and then used voice-over to explain the steps to solve the problem.

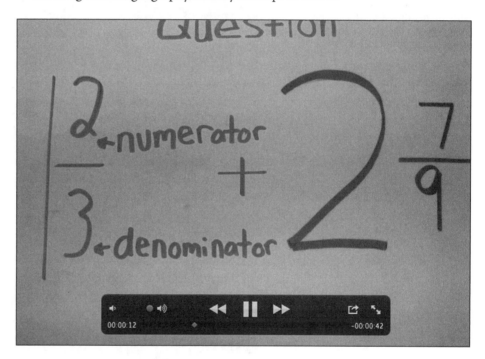

- As a commercial to share an important message, or to share a recommendation about a favorite book.
- Demonstrating their knowledge in a talk-show format through questions and answers.
- Creating documentaries about historical moments, natural disasters, current issues.
- Reenacting a historical time period or important historical moment by role-playing the important personalities.
- Video documentation of changes over time: e.g., the seasons, a step-by-step demonstration of a class experiment.
- As a biography of a real person (artist, scientist, author, historical figure) or of a character in a story.
- As a sportscast or live news piece.
- As a how-to video for playing a game or following directions.

Using Stop-Motion Animation

Stop-motion is an engaging way to create a movie by using images that are presented in series quickly. As the image is slightly altered in each frame, when the frames are put together they create the sense of movement. In print form, the technology exists in the form of flip books. However, using digital tools makes stop-motion accessible for younger students, and the almost magical effect of movement appeals to older students as well.

These screenshots show movement in stop-motion animation in a geometry lesson by teacher Tom Sharpe. Students used shapes from the SMART Board gallery along with the Record feature to touch and move objects on the screen. When Play is clicked on, the movement is reenacted as a movie.

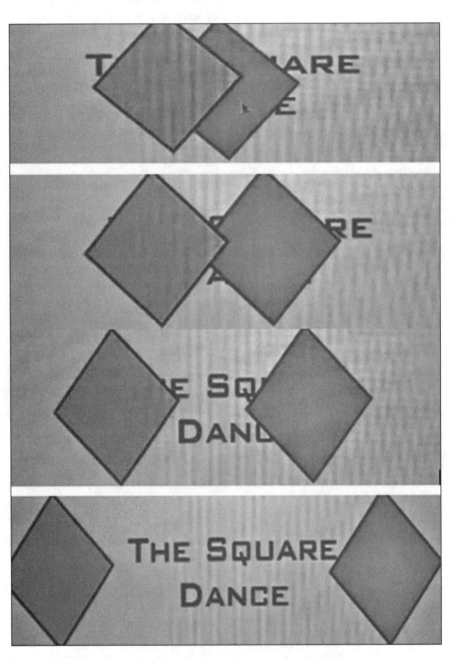

When teaching stop-motion, break the concepts into scenes that will tell a story. What message are students sending and how will they show it? A storyboard is a useful tool to plan a stop-motion video. Once the planning is complete, you can use a variety of digital tools to create stop-motion animation:

- Taking a series of photographs and putting them in a movie-making program that moves though the photos rapidly.
- Taking the same series of photos and downloading them into a Web 2.0 stop-motion application.
- Using the Record option of the IWB. This is the easiest method, especially for young children. Using the IWB, you do not need to take multiple photos, but can create the same effect by slightly altering digital pictures or created graphics. Students post their graphics and then press Record. By moving the graphic just a bit and pressing Record and then Stop, again and again, a stop-motion animation is created.
- Using clay for claymation movies. The same process as for other stop-motion animation is followed: students plan out the steps of the story; they make the characters and scenes using clay; they move the clay slightly, taking a photo with each movement; they put the series of photos together at a rapid pace to create a claymation movie.

This screenshot shows a claymation video by a junior student in the class of Connie vanRijn. The clay is altered very slowly and each change is captured on film. The photos are put together and music or voice-over is added to create a video.

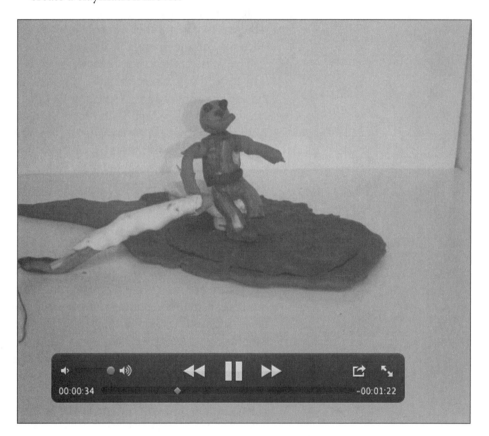

Creating with Web 2.0 Tools

Our students talk about and use Web 2.0 tools like blogs, wikis, and videocasts, but what are they? The Internet began in the 1990s as a means of sharing information. Since web pages were relatively difficult to create (requiring many codes), the Internet was mainly used for reading information and simple communication. By 2000, the Internet had become more user-friendly and demand for it increased. In 2003, the term "Web 2.0" was coined to redefine the Internet as a tool for interacting. Sites like Wikipedia, YouTube, and Facebook changed the way information was presented and shared. The Internet is no longer an authority; now it is a forum where anyone can add, change, interact, blog, and share information. Everyone has become a contributor to the creation of knowledge, making the whole concept collaborative, creative, and innovative.

The way we share information using Web 2.0 changes the way our students think and create. As our world expands, we have the tools to become more connected and add many more layers of information to our existing knowledge. We use Twitter and blogs to get our ideas out there, and these tools are now considered places to access primary sources of information in classes. A blog by a politician or a soldier Tweeting from the front lines of a conflict on the other side of the world share valuable information that adds to our knowledge base. Teachers also contribute to the growth and developement of wikis, podcasts, and moodles. We give feedback through comments and we share videos and photos. We create presentations differently and for larger audiences. This is the world of digital natives and this is the generation we are educating. To capture their ideas, students need more then just a piece of paper and a pencil. They need opportunities to think around, inside, and outside the box, and we need to take the box apart to rebuild it to add another dimension. Web 2.0 tools create an opportunity for this learning, and the interactive whiteboard is a tool to enhance the creative process.

The IWB acts as a tool to showcase Web 2.0 tools. Many Web 2.0 tools do not transfer well onto a piece of paper, but with the IWB you can move fluidly though the various applications. You can touch the screen to pause a moving piece. You can use the pens to highlight information and add comments for your own use. You can bookmark your favorite sites to return to. You can take a screenshot of an effective model to reflect on while you are making your own. The IWB helps you demonstrate and interact with Web 2.0 tools.

Blogs

Blogs are websites or parts of a website where anyone can add their thoughts, comments, or ideas. Using the IWB, you can decipher the blog, model how to comment, and guide your students while they share their ideas locally or globally. There are many free blog sites created for education, such as KidBlog and EduBlog. The IWB creates a safe space for blog entries, as you can monitor students' submissions and authentically teach digital etiquette. You can use a class blog to

- Prompt a discussion to further your class lesson.
- Have students post a question or comment. This could be an assignment with a weekly roster.
- Post review notes for an upcoming assessment piece.
- Post evaluation criteria for assignments completed at home.
- Post a weekly calendar and special events to track what is happening at school.
- Link a blog posting to the next day's discussion by bringing up the site on the IWB.

Moodles©

Moodles were originally created for teachers. Moodle is an open-source learning management system that needs to be hosted and maintained by an IT department. At the most basic level, a Moodle is a private class website that isolates student work from the rest of the Internet, and allows students to use a variety of Web 2.0 tools such as blogging, chatting, or creating a wiki. The Moodle environment is safe and secure. Moodles can also be used to organize your classroom routines, such as homework and calendar, and to clarify rules, such as how to handle an absence. Students can upload photos, video, and audio files. You can also monitor and track student usage. You can attach files that can be downloaded at home and students can submit assignments directly to the Moodle. Opening the Moodle on the IWB at the end of each day replaces the routine of writing down homework to be transfered into an agenda. By streamlining the routine, you can use this valuable time to reflect on a student's thoughtful questions or finish the day with a community circle to reflect on the day and student learning.

Prezis©

The term Prezi is used generically; however, there are various other free Web 2.0 sites that help create dynamic presentations. Preezo, Empressr, Slide Share, Slide, Film Loop, Sliderocket, and Spresent are some examples, and more are appearing all the time.

Just as we use Web 2.0 tools for communicating and collaborating, we can also use them for creating. To replace the traditional slide show, we can create a Prezi, a dynamic and creative tool for presenting information that is available online. Students begin a Prezi with teacher guidance, adding single words or graphics, and presenting information by linking their ideas and zooming in and out of the presentation. Using the IWB, the process of creating a Prezi becomes collaborative as well as engaging. Many concepts become clearer in this format. For example, students learn about what type size means in Prezi, and learn to prioritize the importance of ideas as major or minor. The focus on writing in sentences and short notes forces the creator to think critically and sort information into big ideas and smaller ideas.

Podcasts

For an easy podcast solution, try http://vocaroo.com. This free site enables students to record their voices and then e-mail the file without requiring software.

For students who hesitate to participate in formal presentations and prefer to present information informally, with many practices and drafts, podcasts can bring out their voice. A podcast is an audio file where voices are recorded and saved. Students can create a mini newsfeed about an important issue or share their knowledge and skills. There are various podcasting Web 2.0 tools that make the creation process simple. On many Web 2.0 podcast sites, students can attach their audio documentary or imaginative piece to a visual clip (any graphic, video, photo) to create a richer presentation on the IWB.

Videocasting

Videocasting is the video version of a podcast. Various Web 2.0 tools offer free videocasting, where you can broadcast live video footage. You can also record a video and then upload it later. With this tool, parents can be digitally invited to be part of school events, such as their children presenting at an assembly. Students can also upload a video project that demonstrates their learning.

VoiceThreads©

VoiceThreads© is a website that instantly connects students visually. You can select which topics you want your students to participate in. Once they are ready, students can add their comments to someone's presentation through video, audio, or doodling. You can pause, rewind, or fast forward a video clip to make comments. You can also register your class to create a safe local practice forum prior to allowing students to interact globally. Modeling or using a VoiceThread on the IWB offers your students a strong visual and allows them to interact in a monitored setting.

Traditional

Traditional creative tasks involve traditional tools (paper and pencil, markers, glue) to create. Students might all be assigned the same project or slight variations thereof. There is a lot of erasing and tossing out of first drafts if the students aren't happy with their initial work; having to start over can be demoralizing.

IWB Advantage

There is nothing traditional about teachers who are already using Web 2.0 tools to create and share with their students. The IWB offers a new dynamic to those already comfortable with technology. With the IWB, you can showcase how to use a new Web 2.0 tool. You can model and students can interact with it together. You can experiment by dragging ideas around or by clicking on the various options to learn more about the tools.

An Interactive Idea for Poetry Sharing

Objective
To create a class poem interactively and then bring it to life with sound and visuals; to encourage safe critical thought about the presentation.

Hook
- Read a poem that you feel has appeal for the class.
- Provide students with access to a sampling of poems (through books or the Internet). Allow them time to explore and browse through the poetry. Post the poetry on blank templates on the IWB and save the whole file so students can access it later as they decide on their favorite poems. Create links so students can have the poems read to them.
- Discuss topics for student poetry. Use the IWB to write down brainstormed ideas and then vote and erase the least popular until you decide on a single topic.

Lesson
1. Have each student think of a line, phrase, or sound effect that reflects how he or she feels about the topic. Each student records that idea on the IWB.
2. Bring up the document with all of the students' writing. Clone this document several times for smaller groups to work with.
3. Each group can drag ideas, put them in order, and play with the font for dramatic effect.
4. Give the groups time to practice reading the poem with intonation and fluency. They can access a reading in the poetry file on the IWB to support their practice.
5. Have each group create a visual to complement the poem.
6. Post the groups' visuals on VoiceThreads. Have students read their poems into the microphone on the page with their poem.

---

7. Send students the link to VoiceThreads or keep the site open in the classroom. Reflect on how the same text and topic can be interpreted in many different ways.

8. Encourage students to add positive comments to each other's poetry by opening up an interactive comments page on the IWB and demonstrating how to access it. Have generic comments available as prompts or for struggling writers to simply drag and drop into a comment box to share with another student.

Closure

Use the IWB to share the poetry and the comments on a quiet day when students can sit back and enjoy the poetry and their peers' feedback.

Wikis

As we become more globally connected, our understanding of various issues broadens. We are constantly creating, collaborating, and redefining our understanding of our world. Wikis are tools that create shared definitions. On a wiki, anyone can add information or delete it (sometimes with the permission of the wiki's designer). Looking at one wiki, such as Wikipedia, your students can critically analyze the content of the information. To assess their knowledge, bring them to a wiki on the topic you are learning about. Is the wiki accurate? Would students alter or add anything?

Creating a class wiki gives students a safe place to create definitions and understanding of concepts. A wiki could be used

• To create a class definition list for a geometry unit in math.
• As an individual project, where a student defines terms in a unit of study.
• As a group project, where peers interact and publish their understanding of science concepts.
• To post group work and have students share their feedback on each other's projects.
• To collaboratively create and edit a classroom newspaper.
• By students to post words they find interesting or are stuck finding a meaning for. Peers can add insight and ideas on the meaning of the words.

The IWB acts as a large display where you can open the wiki, model it for the students, and then create a link so that students can update the wiki during a free moment or during centre work.

Word Clouds

A creative way to play with language is to make word clouds with a piece of text. There are a variety of websites that offer this technique. To make a word cloud, students paste their text into the box. They can use a blog or other online source. An image is created by the computer system using the text. The more often a word is used, the bigger the word appears.

Word clouds are great for critical thinking. From a quick glance, we can see the main ideas (the really big words), supporting ideas (smaller words), and details (small words). Word clouds capture the essence of the message by using the dominant words. With them, students can

- Copy and paste speeches from political leaders, famous people, or friends. The big words will represent the ideas they are stressing. This provides a strong visual to see the essence of the message in the speech. If we create word clouds for various people, you can compare their main ideas and see what they believe (e.g., comparing two political leaders and their speeches).
- Copy and paste a text they have written to see if it is sending the message they intend.

This screenshot is a word cloud from wordle.net of a report on Jacques Cartier. Teacher Lisa Fleming and the student could see from this that "exploring," "France," and "Canada" are the important ideas in his work.

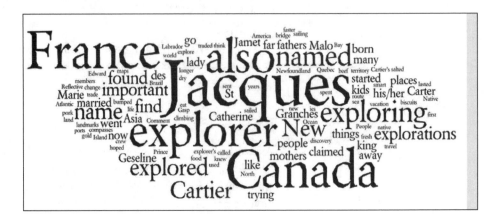

Students can modify a word cloud by deleting words that they feel are not fair representations. They can interact with the visual effects by changing the layout, font, color, and orientation. They can ultimately customize their own word clouds to represent their thoughts, opinions, and beliefs.

Subject-Specific Web 2.0 Tools

In addition to the general Web 2.0 tools that can be applied to any topic we teach, there are Web 2.0 tools that directly relate to specific subjects. There are Web 2.0 tools for creating a graph (NCES Kids Graphs), translating web pages (lingo), solving and explaining math problems (Mathway), mapping and visualizing a community (CommunityWalk), creating personal maps (Wayfaring)—there are even sites to make music and mix colors. If your students can imagine it, then you can most likely find a Web 2.0 tool that will bring their ideas to life. Not only can you use the IWB to model these specific tools, but you can also set up a direct link on your browser for your students to easily access the sites and practice using them at home or at independent centres.

The Web 2.0 tools we use can interact with each other. Further tools exist that can combine blogging, video, photos, and wikis. You can share all of your ideas using the variety of options available. Once students have created a digital file, their options for sharing multiply. A traditional poster can sit in the hallway and then move into Mom and Dad's office. But a podcast, a Prezi, a wiki, or any Web 2.0 tool can be e-mailed, played on a DVD player, or linked to a class or school web page to be shared and enjoyed by many, anywhere in the world. You can videotape student presentations and add this piece of digital media to their portfolios or as a holiday gift for parents. The IWB can showcase students' work during conferences and, just as any assessment piece, it can act evidence of student learning. Combining the IWB with Web 2.0 tools creates a classroom rich in digital media and an environment for engaged and authentic learning.

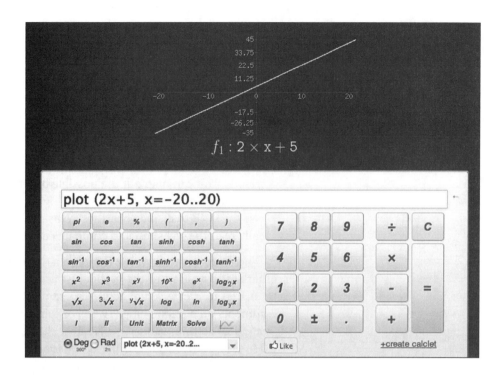

This screenshot demonstrates a math Web 2.0 tool found at http://web2.0calc.com. It is a graphing calculator students can use to instantly translate numbers and equations into a graph.

Taking Action on Our Learning

Learning is enhanced and remembered meaningfully when students are able to demonstrate their understanding in a new or novel way. We spend hours teaching our students to read, hoping that they will pick up a book on their own with sheer eagerness or apply their knowledge practically by reading an information sign or instructions. When students alter their regular routines to incorporate their recent learning, they are taking action. If students stop before throwing out a piece of paper, or put seeds out for birds in the winter, they have personally taken action. As Herbert Spencer said, "The great aim of education is not knowledge, but action."

Creating Social Action

"What you leave behind is not what is engraved in stone monuments, but what is woven into the lives of others."
—Pericles

When our students take initiative to demonstrate their knowledge in a manner that influences others, they are engaged in social action. Social action is a meaningful and authentic way for students to participate in the local or global community. Ultimately, we are educating students so that they positively affect our world. Teaching them to act with empathy and caring for others in the world is an important part of preparing students for their futures. Social action can be as big as a global campaign for change or as small as a letter to a solider, as long as our students are trying to affect others. Social action projects for students can be wide ranging and easily incorporate digital technology and the IWB. Our students can

- Prepare a speech, song, or play; record it; and then visit a seniors home where they can present. They can give the seniors a DVD or CD to be replayed.
- Compose a card or graphic to cheer up someone in the hospital.
- E-mail thank-you campaigns: e.g., to astronauts, authors, or soliders in a different part of the world

- Create an information campaign about an important topic, such as safety or recycling, using Web 2.0 tools such as blogs to share information with the school or local community.
- Collect food for food banks following a nutrition unit. You can follow up with the food bank or charity by asking for photos or sharing an e-mail on the large screen so that students are aware of the impact they have.
- Compile interview video clips from guest speakers and share the information with others in the school.
- Create a poster to advertise a charity event and send it digitally to parents and friends. You can map out the possible broadening of the message and how it can reach many people quickly.
- Use the IWB to display charities' websites: students suggest the charites, critically read the websites, and compare each charity until one is selected.

There are various Web 2.0 tools that can instantly connect our students to other students around the globe. Just as any presentation on bristol board can be shared to create social action, so can any Web 2.0 tool. Once students type comments on a public blog, Tweet, or join a social network, they are interacting in a global setting. When you create a class blog or wiki, you are using the Web 2.0 tool in a private and secure space for the purpose of learning about the tool and using the tool to enhance learning. When you access a public blog or wiki, you instantly connect globally, and your participation can be a social action. It is important to teach students the difference between a secure site created for learning and a public site that anyone can access. Once students have an understanding of the possibilities, the concept of social action becomes authentic, as they eagerly want to share their opinions or ideas on a "real" public website. Using the IWB, you can monitor their contribution and use it as a springboard for authentic teaching.

6

The IWB as a Tool For Assessment

Just as the interactive whiteboard is a tool for learning, it also can have impact on assessment processes—what we assess and how we assess it. Traditionally, it has been common practice to have students fill in a sheet or complete a test or assignment that is check-marked and graded for accuracy at the end of learning. It seems much more difficult to assess how students perform, think, interact, and problem solve during the learning. Assessing student knowledge prior to, during, and when ending a unit can be challenging. The IWB can assist with all three in a meaningful way to support assessment *for*, *as*, and *of* learning.

The IWB allows teachers to save and revisit student products to assess progress of both knowledge and skills as our students learn. It is a place where students can work collaboratively to solve problems. Listening in on a small group working at the IWB is an important part of assessment. Having "butterfly conferences" with students—where teachers engage in short conversations about learning, ask questions, prompt, and listen for responses—are crucial assessment to support learning. Finally, the IWB is able to record responses, compile "right" answers, and give teachers information about content students might be struggling with. When the teacher clones an activity, each student (or group) can complete and save the same activity, and the teacher can use the contents of a folder as assessment pieces. These files can be used as a stepping stone to the next learning activity or as a formal document that can be used or shared in report cards or parent conferences. When you are modeling a lesson, you can explain why you are doing what you are doing or share the learning goals. This allows your students to internalize a process. When it is their time to complete a task, you can then ask them to think about the process they are following and critically examine what works best for their learning, thereby creating success criteria that they can use to support their own learning.

Learning is a process; therefore, to best detemine what to teach, where to go next, and what our students ultimately know is a subject that has been researched by many. There are common educational terms that refer to the assessment processes in classrooms. Assessment *for*, *as,* and *of* learning are the terms developed and used by researchers, ministries of education, and teachers to help us navigate our students' learning and understand how best to teach them (Earl, 2006):

- Assessment *for* learning is designed to give teachers information that will allow them to modify the teaching and learning activities in which students are engaged, in order to differentiate and understand how individual students approach their learning.
- Assessment *as* learning is a subset of assessment for learning that emphasizes using assessment as a process of developing and supporting metacognition for students. Assessment *as* learning focuses on the role of the student as the critical connector between assessment and learning.

- Assessment *of* learning is used to confirm what students know, to demonstrate whether or not the students have met the standards and/or show how they are placed in relation to others.

These assessment strategies and tools can be used with the IWB:
- Direct observation
- Interest Inventories/Checklists: can be filled out directly on the IWB and saved. Data can be transformed into graphs for grouping or comparison purposes.
- Journals (personal, reading response, and dialogue journals; math or science journals): for sharing knowledge and receiving descriptive feedback from peers and teacher
- Performance tasks
- Games that give immediate feedback
- Performance standards, rubrics, benchmarks, success criteria: can be collaboratively and interactively developed by teacher and students
- Portfolios of student work: collaboratively and interactively created by teacher and student

Assessment *For* Learning

Assessment for learning, otherwise known as diagnostic or formative assessment, is a process that involves the ongoing gathering and interpreting of information about what students know and can do. The information from assessment for learning is used by teachers to adjust instruction and provide feedback to students to support learning. Assessment for learning can have a very positive impact on student learning and achievement. Clear targets are set by sharing criteria from assessment, students are shown models of quality work, and activities encourage reflection, self-assessment, and setting learning goals. Students are given feedback as well as ongoing assessment that is not evaluative but is intended to guide learning.

The following questions help teachers and students focus their thinking as they assess for learning. Teachers should ask themselves
- What is the student demonstrating he/she knows and is able to do?
- So, what feedback will I provide?
- Now, what further instruction/guidance is required?

Students should ask themselves
- What do I know already?
- What am I interested in learning more about?

See Chapter 5 for more on KWL and RAN organizers.

An important starting point for planning assessment is to understand students' prior knowledge when beginning a unit of study. Ask your students to share their knowledge. Brainstorm ideas with them using an organizer, such as a KWL or RAN organizer. When you use the IWB to save students' thoughts and demonstrations of prior knowledge as a document, it allows students to add to, change, and delete information and to demonstrate how their understandings have changed over time. The original brainstorm document also acts as a strong tool to demonstrate growth as the end of a unit of study, to show students where they started. Each student can have a brainstorming web or chart that they can add to and modify throughout a unit, and that can be displayed on the IWB to share, give feedback, and set goals. Newer versions can be saved by dating the file name; files can be used to demonstrate growth over time. Be sure to allow students to experiment, share opinions, explore, and even make mistakes! With the IWB, mistakes are less frightening because of the "errorless" nature of the board. It is easy for a student to move or delete an idea, picture, or word and create a product more representative of that student's current thinking.

Feedback

Feedback is not meant to be simply a grade or positive word at the top of a test. Feedback is an essential part of assessment for learning. Given to students in a timely, focused way, it has a positive impact on student learning. Feedback must be frequent and give students clear direction in relation to their progress and goals.

Traditional

Traditionally, feedback in a classroom is available only from teacher or peers. Students work at tasks without receiving feedback, receive feedback sporadically, or are given general comments to motivate them to keep working. Teachers typically also give summative feedback at the end of a task in the form of a grade or description of strengths, needs, and next steps.

IWB Advantage

Feedback offers opportunities for assessment *for* and *as* learning. An important aspect of the IWB is its ability to give immediate feedback as students move closer to attaining learning goals set by themselves and the teacher. Young people are engaged in video games for long periods of time because video games are set up to give immediate feedback. A game player who takes a shot in a sports game knows instantly if that shot scored. If the player did not score, he or she is given the opportunity to try something else; therefore, players get a better understanding of how to move closer to the goal set out in the game. Immediate feedback is a crucial part of learning. The IWB is full of possibilities for immediate feedback— from simple games (which can be accessed on the Internet) for practicing skills, to programs that allow you to set up systems for giving immediate, accurate, authentic feedback to your learners. You can use a premade template, such as a multiple-choice quiz, or you can create your own. Through games, students can respond, sort, and move objects to represent their understandings; the IWB will tell students if they are right/wrong, will tally up their scores, will give them hints about what to try, and will even tell them if they're doing a great job!

An Interactive Idea for Immediate Feedback

Objective
To strengthen students' basic math skills.

Hook
Give students the opportunity to throw a koosh ball at the IWB to spark interest and attention.

Lesson
1. Create a review game board with various circles that each link to a separate page (or download the Koosh Ball Template from www.exchange.smarttech. com). On each page, write a math equation.
2. Now the fun begins! Armed with a koosh ball, each student throws the ball at the IWB. When a student hits a circle, it directly links to a math equation for that student to answer.
3. With students taking turns, you can complete a full math review in a matter of minutes in an interactive and engaging way.

Closure
Once the review is complete, have students delete the questions they found too easy and replace them with more appropriate questions for next time.

This screenshot shows a template for sorting, created by teacher Lara Jensen on a SMART Board, that has been individualized for a group of students learning vowel sounds. Unlike a worksheet, this template allows students to check their work, reset to try again, and click on Solve to help them with the difficult examples. Once students have completed the task, they can click on Edit to add more visuals for the next group.

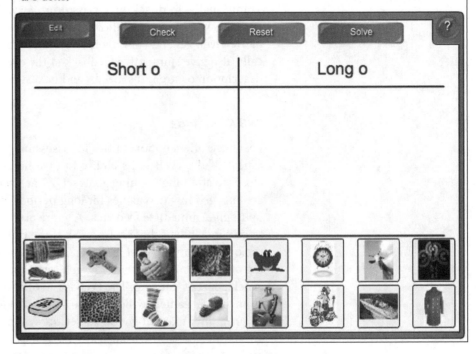

Look at the pictures and think about what it is showing. Is it showing a word with a long o or a short o sound?
Drag the picture to the correct side of the chart. Check your work when you are done.

Descriptive feedback involves sharing thoughts and ideas, usually in oral or written form, to support learners to reach goals. Descriptive feedback can be positive, and gives students personalized next steps. This type of feedback can also be given using an IWB. A student's work can be displayed on the IWB, and peers and teachers can use different colored pens to "mark up" the work, giving short descriptive feedback focused on the student's learning goals. The criteria for assessment can be displayed beside the student's work to ensure the feedback is specific to the piece of work. Different criteria can be viewed for different work samples by simply accessing the appropriate file and displaying the criteria side-by-side with the work sample. You can also provide feedback in class blogs, wikis, and websites where your students share their ongoing learning.

Student Response System for Assessment

The student response system, or clickers, were developed for IWBs for the purpose of assessment. They are an effective tool to determine what students know and what needs to be reviewed. The system involves a few key items:

- Handheld clickers that students use to key in responses
- Templates and programming for the clickers in the IWB program
- Results data: These data are produced by the clickers, in chart and graph form. They are available for students and teacher to analyze and discuss. Teachers can use this information to adapt teaching.

This screenshot shows how the clickers share information on a SMART Board after a question has been answered. The question is displayed side-by-side with the results. The IWB has tallied how many students answered correctly and has provided a graph of the results. This graph can be easily converted into a bar graph.

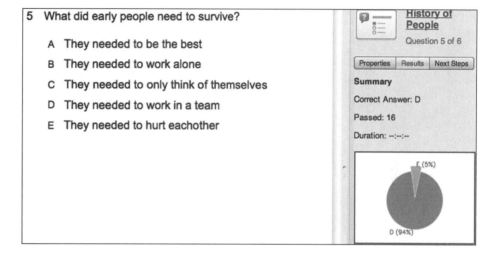

The system can provide you with details about your students' learning. Begin by using the templates to create a quiz for students on any given topic. Once you have designed the quiz, give each student a clicker. The students can select the class and quiz. The results can remain anonymous, or students can select their name on the list (which you program for them) and record their own individual results. Post the questions on the IWB and have students respond with their clickers. From this, you can collect data. You can find out who knows what, who needs more help, and what needs to be retaught. Graphs can be displayed instantly (without names). The clickers have many advantages for assessment.

The IWB allows for variety in the student response system. While planning and giving the quiz, you can

- Use a variety of question styles: multiple choice, true/false, yes/no, multiple answer.
- Determine how many questions (up to 40), what you want to ask, and how much each question is worth; or you can set up questions that ask for students' opinions.
- Design quizzes with words, graphics, or sound, with the same flexibility that you use to create lessons on an IWB document.
- Pace the lesson to provide students with enough wait time; quizzes can be timed for speed drills.
- Write or explain ideas using the pens, flipping between other pages in class files, or referring to prior activities saved on the computer.

Students can
- Remain at their seats, anonymously interacting with the IWB at the same time. Students can also work from any area of the classroom using the clicker if, for example, one student is having difficulty focusing in the whole-class setting.
- Access the question aurally and visually; i.e., you can read it, or have it read for the auditory component.

When reflecting on the results, you can
- Provide students and yourself with instant feedback about what students really know.
- Know which students understand the concept.
- Find out who is really struggling, so you can start to target ways to help that student succeed.
- Reflect on your assessment data in many formats: bar graph, pie graph, chart of names listing students' results.

Assessment *As* Learning

Assessment *as* learning is concerned with the role of the student during the assessment process. It develops students' metacognition, as they participate actively in the assessment process. In assessment as learning, students monitor their own learning and use assessment feedback from the teacher and peers to set learning goals. The process requires students to have a clear understanding of both the learning goals and the criteria for success.

These questions can help students and teachers focus their thinking as they participate in assessment as learning processes. Students should ask themselves:
- How can I connect what I am learning to what I already know?
- What am I demonstrating I know or am able to do?
- So what does feedback mean for me?
- Now what do I need to do next? What are my learning goals?

You should ask yourself:
- What feedback will I continue to provide?
- What further instruction/guidance is required?

For this screenshot, Lara Jensen's students began by brainstorming what they knew about games/sports and dance. The ideas were placed in each category of the Venn on a SMART Board. As they experienced and "played" dance, they came up to the IWB to move their earlier ideas around and add new ideas. In the end, the students determined that games/sports and dance share the same attributes.

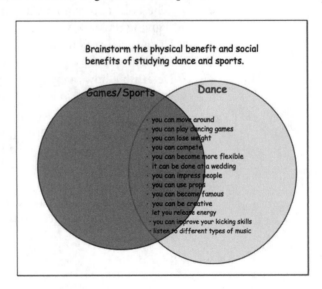

These assessment-as-learning strategies and tools can be used with the IWB:
- Student-involved assessment
- Rubrics: brief statements based on components/criteria to describe achievement at different levels
- Student self-assessment or peer-assessment tools: students reflecting on their own learning

Using the IWB, you can support students as they self-assess during the learning process by
- Teaching them to how to track changes on writing software. This shows them how they have altered the original piece and keeps a record of their progress.
- Posting a problem on a blog for a homework assignment or as part of a lesson. Have students record their original ideas and then collaborate as a class on the blog to find a solution. By reflecting on their preconceived notions, students become aware of their learning process.
- Posting an experiment or concept on the IWB, along with learning goals and criteria for success. Have students complete the physical activity and then share their results on the IWB.
- Creating a word cloud to determine what words they are using the most and to see the essence of the message they are sending.

See Chapter 5 for more on word clouds.

In this screenshot, Kindergarten students used the IWB to track their learning during science stations. As they experimented with different materials, they worked together to decide which category each object fit in. They can go back to test again, share their experiments with peers, and wonder why, easily changing their original response if they change their minds. (Images courtesy of SMART Technologies.)

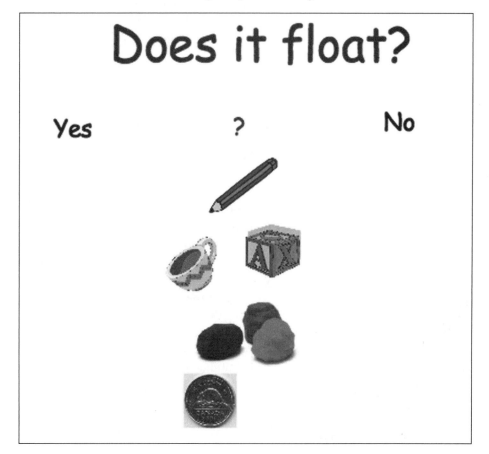

Assessment *Of* Learning

This type of assessment involves the process of collecting evidence for the purpose of summarizing learning at a point in time. Assessment of learning is usually done with reference to a set of criteria, and evaluative judgments are made about the quality of student learning. This is a key part of the assessment process, as it usually results in grades and evaluation of final products for reporting.

Assessment-of-learning strategies and tools include
- Tests
- Culminating tasks with rubrics
- Criteria for evaluation
- Written products (stories, essays)

These questions help teachers and students focus their thinking as evaluate progress, knowledge, and skills. Students should ask themselves:
- What do I feel I have learned?
- What can I do with this knowledge? How will this knowledge inform my actions?

You should ask yourself:
- *What* is the student demonstrating he/she knows and is able to do?
- *So what* do these results tell me about the student's developing strengths?
- *Now what* are the next steps?

Performance Tasks/Products: Sharing and Assessing Student Learning

We have endless options when deciding how to evaluate our students' learning. Performance tasks are ways of assessing learning that are not "completing a sheet" or "writing a test." In performance tasks, students apply the skills and knowledge they have learned in a unit of study to create a product. One of the best ways to motivate students to learn is by designing a unit-culminating task that allows students to choose how they want to share their knowledge and create a product that represents their understanding. There are many ways to share learning:
- Using an application to create a slide show
- Using a movie-making application to record a dramatic scene
- Creating and sharing a photo, a slide show, music, or video
- Using a timeline or flow chart to demonstrate a linear process or chronology
- Using the endless bank of graphics and art tools (pens, color, shapes) to create murals or visual representations of ideas
- Posting a large blank template of a picture dictionary and having students add definitions or ideas as the unit progresses, or as an end-of-unit task
- Creating a museum exhibit to sort and display newly gained knowledge
- Using photo programs to create digital scrapbooks showcasing ideas and photos; using the Pens tools to convert photos into diagrams with labels

This screenshot shows an assessment tool developed in Filemaker Pro for a choice-based art class of teacher Connie vanRijn. Each student has a page. Verbal reflections are captured on a podcaster. Using photos and the verbal reflections of her students' work, the teacher can track art work, listen to student voices, and reflect and report on progress in a deep and authentic way.

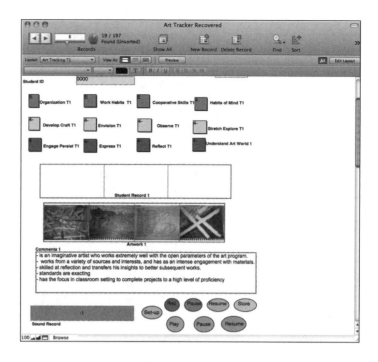

Traditional

Using paper, glue, and scissors, students create poster boards, dioramas, or art pieces. They can write a speech, prepare a skit, or sing a song. All of these projects take time, demonstrate knowledge, and allow students to practice skills.

IWB Advantage

The IWB can help bring our students' performance tasks to life. In creating a simple slide show, the discomfort a student might feel about a public speech is lessened, as the presenter can control the slide show by interacting directly with the presentation. The presenter can flip through the show while talking, using the visuals as a cuing system. If students create a piece of digital media, the IWB is the ideal display. Digital media products are easily shared when they are placed on a USB and inserted into the computer. Students can confidently click and move through their presentation without worrying about looking at a computer or the hook-up. Using the IWB, students' presentation skills are strengthened and the product looks polished.

An Interactive Idea for Assessment

We can connect our students' knowledge of technology with our classroom learning in an engaging way by using what they know and love. Rather than a character analysis of a protagonist or a historical figure, why not create a social media page for that character?

Objective
To assess our students' understanding of a historical figure.

Hook
Preview a social media site (e.g., Facebook) with the students and walk through the various aspects: profile, comments, friends, photos. Use a critical

---

lens to demonstrate and show how every aspect of the page connects to the person, even the advertising. This activity must be facilitated by a teacher in order to guide students through the critical thinking necessary to view the content involved social media; see Chapter 4 and the section on Netiquette.

Lesson

1. Provide students with a template of a blank social media page. There are now websites that copy the style of Facebook to make this process easier (e.g., www.myfakewall.com).

2. It is the students' job to create a social media page for their historical character. They will need to critically think about what photo the character might select, who would be that character's friends, what the character would post in a profile, and what comments the character might write. Students can get creative, adding advertisements that are historically correct and fit the character's profile.

3. Students can view the constructed page on the IWB in small groups, decide together how to change or modify it, and assign tasks. They can drag ideas from one section to another, discuss, and then move again. They can e-mail it and work independently or collaboratively on a laptop or desktop.

Closure

The students can share their pages with each other by inviting others as friends. Students will need to preview other sites to determine if the characters would have been friends, and invite, accept, or reject with a historical justification.

By using the digital format for sharing learning, our students are instantly engaged. Our students know that they can make mistakes and simply shift or delete the previous attempt, creating a more polished product and gaining critical self-editing skills. They are eager to use digital media because it creates a clean and professional product that is appealing. They can focus on the big ideas such as collecting their knowledge, organizing their ideas, and determining how to best apply their knowledge into the digital media.

Performance tasks, just like a traditional worksheet or test, require planning on the part of teachers. When designing any performance task

- Be sure the project allows students to demonstrate knowledge and understanding.
- Make it authentic. Students should have a real reason for creating the product.
- Provide opportunities to share the products outside the classroom walls.
- Make sure there is the opportunity for choice; there must be a number of different ways to complete the project, depending on the learner.
- Allow opportunities for students to work in groups, but also ways to demonstrate knowledge and skills as individuals. Group and individual assessment are both possible within the framework of performance tasks.

Assessment and Critical Thinking

Graphic Organizers

Critical thinking is strengthened when students are given the opportunity to use graphic organizers to demonstrate knowledge or understanding and to communicate their ideas. Returning to saved files where ideas were organized, you have a collection of information about your students' prior knowledge and new learning. For a quick assessment trick, clone the page where students brainstormed what they already knew. Individually, in small groups, or as a whole class, have students cross out inaccuracies, expand beginning ideas, and add more ideas. This alone is an assessment tool. Using graphic organizers, students share knowledge of concepts and their thinking.

The interactive nature of the IWB supports students as they think critically or specifically to analyze, evaluate, or synthesize information. With the IWB, you can use graphic organizers as an assessment tool by having students

- Sort information into a flow chart, such as a timeline or ranking ladder, where they need to place the information into a specific order based on time or importance.

This screenshot shows an activity created by teacher Sarah Barclay using Inspiration®, for which the students needed to organize the provinces and territories of Canada by name and then add the capital city. The flags (images courtesy of SMART Technologies) provided a visual link.

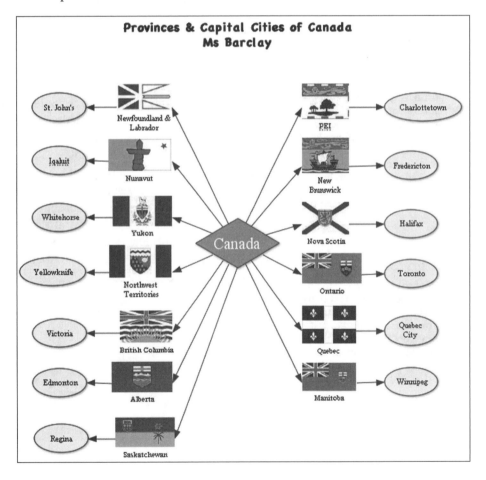

- Classify and sort information into organizers for higher-level thinking:

Fishbone diagram: used to organize information from the big ideas to the supporting details; the head of the fish states the issue or focus of thinking, in the squares are the main ideas, and off the squares are examples of the main idea.

In this screenshot, students were given the words and required to drag and sort the information. In more complex examples, you can use information created in prior lessons to drag and sort. Students can also determine what should and should not be included in their fishbone, justifying their response.

```
            Wind              Water
                  -wind turbines    -hydroelectric dams
                                    -tidal power
Sources of
Renewable
Energy
                  -solar panels     -heat pumps
                  -solar radiation  -hot springs
            Solar             Geothermal
```

Concept map: starts with a major term or theme at the top, shifts from more-complex to less-complex ideas, and ends with an example of each; connecting lines are drawn between concepts and linking words are placed on the lines, stating relationship between concepts.

Mind map: begins with a central image representing the subject being mapped; main themes and branches radiate outward, with images or words printed on interconnected branches.

Graphic organizers have proven to be successful tools to incorporate critical thinking, as they require us to sort, classify, and synthesize our knowledge. As an assessment tool, they challenge our students to critically think and then visually organize and display their knowledge. IWBs make graphic organizers easy to manipulate and help separate technical skills from critical thinking and application skills. With the IWB as a tool, you can easily move ideas, change color, or add graphic images to complement a concept. You can work collaboratively and view the graphic organizer on the large display as a whole class. You can touch and grab a concept, try it in a different place, and drag it somewhere else if you change your mind. You can save drafts, come back, and apply critical thinking skills at a later point. The IWB helps to decrease the challenge of graphic organizers, allowing you and your students to focus on the big ideas involved in learning.

For online mind-mapping tools, try
Gliffy.com
Exploratree.org.uk
MindMeister.com
Mindomo.com
Bubbl.us
Mappio.com
Text2MindMap.com
Popplet.com

"'Mom, today I made a mind map with Justin,' Nigel shared at dinner. With sincere parental curiosity, Mom asked, 'What is a mind map?' Nigel, exasperated, responded, 'Oh, Mom. It is too difficult to explain, but it is really fun.'"
—Grade 1 moment shared by a parent.

This screenshot is a type of mind map for multiplication created by teacher Lara Jensen using Inspiration®. The students worked on it collaboratively throughout the unit to demonstrate and consolidate their understanding of this concept.

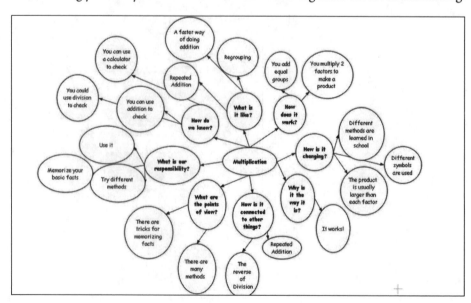

Electronic Portfolios

Now that your students are collaborating, communicating, and creating on the interactive whiteboard, you can use electronic portfolios to save and store their products. You have encouraged students to create digital text with photos, movies, and Web 2.0 tools. They are creating presentations and collaborating at centres. An electronic portfolio is a medium that organizes individual students' learning in a meaningful way. Traditionally, a portfolio is a collection of student work. Pieces are selected and reflected on by the student with goals and criteria as a guide. Since your students are now creating digital media, how do you use the IWB to store, reflect, and share their learning?

To save and store learning, you can

- Create a file for each student on the desktop. As a task is completed, a student can take a screenshot and save in his or her files.
- Create a class folder that houses collective pieces of work; e.g., a class perfomance at an assembly, a collective song, pieces of work created collaboratively.
- Create a template for each student and use the template to organize the portfolio. Pieces can be placed directly into the template and reflected on, using graphics and speech bubbles.
- Use a Web 2.0 tool, such as an individual website, to store learning. Students can add video, sound, and pieces of work, either scanned in or linked. Students can also access their portfolios at home and contribute to an ongoing dialogue about their learning. Parents, teachers, and peers can add comments and reflection.

To reflect on their work, students can

- Retrieve pieces that they have completed. In a word-processing document, they can use tools such as Track Changes or Notes to make comments on their pieces.
- Bring the selected piece of work onto a blank template. They and their peers can comment on the piece with the pens and then take a screenshot of the work with the added input.
- Use podcasts and voice software to incorporate oral reflection in the portfolio.

To share your students' work, you can

- Burn a disk for each student, including the personal folder as well as the class folder.
- E-mail the folder to students directly.
- Post selected pieces on a share site, such as a class wiki, blog, or Moodle.

The electronic portfolio can be a reflection of all digital work or a combination of digital work and scanned non-digital work. The portfolios are individualized for each student and tailored to each students' strengths with the multiple options provided by the IWB and digital technology.

7

Reaching All Students

Our students need carefully planned learning experiences to support their strengths and to address their various needs. In any elementary classroom, there will be students with varied learning styles, linguistic and cultural differences, different motivation levels, and learning exceptionalities. For these students, the interactive whiteboard and digital technology can be powerful tools for learning. The IWB provides many possibilities for inclusion of diverse learners into any classroom.

The power of our digital world is that it creates open access to interactive experiences, situated in the classroom (e.g., software) and across the world (e.g., via the Internet). Technology gives students a sense of ownership and engages learners as they apply their knowledge and problem solve using the digital tools available. With the many resources that exist, you can find tools to accommodate and empower all of your learners. You can open up a world of possibilities as you explore new information together and incorporate the various multimedia available to us. The power of the IWB and digital technology also lies in the ability to save files, assess progress, revise and edit easily, give feedback, and chart new paths based on where students are at and what they need.

As you move from whole-class lessons to small-group and individual use of the IWB, you are also taking a step back from traditional teaching with print. You are empowering your students. However, teachers still have the important role to model for students and guide them toward independence. This chapter steps through the process of addressing the needs of all diverse learners.

Reaching the Whole Class

At the beginning of each school year, new students arrive in our classrooms and we begin the process of engaging them in learning. We have spent the summer preparing, thinking, fearing, and building excitement for this day. It is the day we meet the people that we will spend the better part of a year growing, learning, and exploring with. It is the start of something new.

When beginning to plan for students, we need to address two main areas. The first: Who are our students? What are their interests? Where are their passions and what motivates them? What do they already know and what can they already do? Next, we have to understand how they learn, as teaching is really a response to what we know about learning and learners. Through careful observation and conversations, and standardized or curriculum-based assessments, you can assess your learners and plan for their success. As a class, they have their own dynamic. This dynamic will affect how they cooperate, interact, and learn as a whole.

See Chapter 3 for ideas on whole-class collaboration.

The interactive whiteboard comes into play in our large-group dynamic. From its sheer size and placement, students recognize it as a powerful tool in the classroom and they are keen to use it. It can be used for sharing, organizing, and interacting. You can gather together in the morning, take attendance, and discuss recent news, the weather, or a pressing issue in the classroom or school community. You can model lessons throughout the day. You can watch as students share their learning or model a lesson for you. You can reach beyond classroom walls and connect your class globally, or you can use it to organize your routines and systems inside the classroom.

Research tells us that students learn more effectively when we incorporate their interests in the classroom. By starting with student interests, we are creating positive emotions that support learning for them. We need to think critically about how we are teaching if we expect our students to think critically about what they are learning. Using technology and the IWB, you can teach to using your knowledge of how the brain learns by

- Providing real-world examples in your teaching. You can present the content of your teaching to apply to your students' lives. For a measurement unit, have your students measure, map out, and create a model of a room in their house, or have them design a new room that fits the space and that they like. Using the IWB, they can make scale models and place furniture and other moveable pieces on the model. This allows them to think critically about measurement, scale, and models in an interactive and meaningful way.
- Fully immersing the students in the learning experience, engaging them in hands-on learning, technology, and talk. If the class is learning about electricity, using the IWB to create an interactive game for conductors can be complemented by bringing in a set of conductors for students to use to replicate electrical connections they found interesting. As well, students can do this work in small groups as they negotiate and problem solve together.
- Showcasing and experimenting with a variety of digital tools (computers, IWB, tablets, software, online resources) to help determine what helps a student learn best. This strategy also provides many experiences for students to interact with the content they are learning and helps them retain the taught concepts.

Reaching Small Groups

Just as the interactive whiteboard is useful in whole-class instruction, it is also a tool for small-group interactions. In a small group, students need to work together to navigate who touches the IWB, what the response will be, and how to share the interaction equally. As much as the task they are completing is important, so too is the group interaction that occurs during this process.

See Chapter 3 for more on collaborating in small groups.

The IWB expands the possibilities for learning. It also supports how students interact and collaborate in smaller groupings. Students are provided with instant feedback on activities from the IWB, on websites, and by using the IWB tools, as well as from their peers. Over time, they learn to navigate the responses and learn from each other. The single-touch aspect of the IWB forces collaboration from your students. They need to communicate and cooperate to determine whose turn it is to touch and what everyone has agreed on as the response. For multi-touch whiteboards, students still need to collaborate to collectively decide what they want to produce. Of course, all these procedures must be modeled before setting students up to work in small groups.

Small groups can be used

- During centre work: literacy centres, math centres, or any centres designed for independent work around any content area. Centre work can be part of a rotational cycle or left for the students to explore. The IWB can be easily set up as a centre in the classroom.
- During an activity or lesson. After the lesson has been taught and students break out to practice the skill, you can rotate groups to work on the IWB for practice time. By tracking when they use it, or by using a pre-existing group (e.g., table groups or guided reading groups) as a tracker, you can ensure that everyone gets a chance to use the IWB before the next rotation.
- When a task has been completed. The IWB can be the activity station for students who have completed their work and are now being challenged with extension activities.

Reaching All Individuals

See Chapter 6 for more on assessing for student learning.

We know that ultimately we are responsible for nurturing and guiding each individual student. Therefore, we need instructional and assessment processes that allow us to know what students already know and what they have learned as a result of our instruction. We need to know our learners, who they are, how to reach them, and how to assess their knowledge. We begin by finding out a bit more about our students—individually. How do they learn best?

Incorporating Multiple Modalities

Our classrooms are filled with students who have diverse learning needs. Through the use of multimodal texts, students constantly have opportunities to use linguistic, visual, and auditory modes to make meaning. You can use multiple modalities as an intentional response to what you know about your learners. The more ways you teach, the more modalities you touch upon, the more likely you will be to reach all your students with the IWB. The aim is to move away from traditional teaching practices that favor one modality (e.g., linguistic). The strategies presented here allow students to process information through multiple modalities.

Integrating Visuals

Most learners comprehend and retain information better when presented with visuals, such as graphics or pictures. The IWB is ideal to support this tendency, as it acts as a large visual display. You can easily integrate pictures, charts, graphs, maps, or graphics onto the screen. You can use the IWB to support your visual learners by

- Color coding to highlight important ideas or concepts, such as highlighting all the question words red and the answer prompts blue to prompt a writing piece.
- Incorporating pictures with text.

- Showing how easy it is to manipulate ideas, move them, and reorganize them, possibly into graphic organizers to understand relationships between concepts and recall.
- Designing a whiteboard mosaic to represent ideas, using graphics, magazine cutouts, and single words.
- Using interactive visuals from the software for your IWB, such as the visual timer to time a math speed drill or an interactive clock that shows the parallel movement for digital and analog clocks.

See Chapter 5 for more on graphic organizers.

This screenshot is an example of a concept attainment lesson. In this lesson, a few non-polygon (on the left) examples were drawn and a few polygon (on the right) examples were drawn. The students were required to figure out the rule defining a polygon. If they thought they knew it, they had to prove it by adding a shape to either the left or right side. As more shapes were added, more and more students understood the rule. More shapes were added as testers and students had to determine what went where. Finally, the word "polygon" was spelled out for the category on the right. The rules the students developed became the definition for *polygon*. This file can be saved and can be pulled up as a visual reminder and reference when working on shapes during independent work.

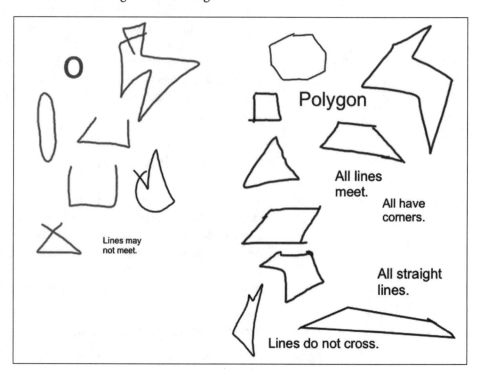

See Chapter 5 for more on podcasts.

Integrating Sound

Moving beyond the single-voice lecture style of teaching, you can use the IWB to support students by

- Presenting music, and tone and pitch variety to grab students' attention and support those who have a preference for sound.
- Linking to podcasts for information on a history unit, and then having students create podcasts to share their ideas.
- Setting up sound cues on your desktop to signal routines; e.g., a clapping sound when a new idea is presented, a whistle for attention, a sweeping noise to clean up the room.
- Conducting an interview/recording a lesson using a Web 2.0 podcast tool or software that records voice.

Integrating Movement

Students often learn more effectively when given the opportunity to move. Our kinesthetic learners are active students who retain concepts more effectively if they are physically moving. Although it might seem as though the entire Kindergarten class is filled with kinesthetic learners, true kinesthetic learners need to move in order to learn. Combined with good teaching, use of the IWB can help support kinesthetic learners by

See Chapter 6 for a koosh ball activity.

- Creating a flow of movement during lessons to engage students to touch the IWB.
- Incorporating games, such as koosh ball, that require students to move their bodies at the IWB to practice skills.
- Creating a role play, videotaping it, and replaying it on the IWB, pausing and interacting with the video.
- Creating a claymation piece to share learning while interacting with technology and developing fine motor skills.
- Working through a simulation. Show one from an online video (such as a car moving) and then have students re-create the movement.
- Creating actions for a song or dramatizing a text that is played on the IWB.
- Posting information that needs to be physically touched to be sorted.

Other Challenges

Beyond learning styles, students come to us with a variety of backgrounds that affect how they learn. We may have students with preferences for linguistic, visual, or kinesthetic approaches in our class. However, due to a language, social, or other barrier, we struggle to reach them as individuals. In our classrooms are a variety of students, and some students require additional support beyond accommodation to their learning styles. We may have students who struggle with the language of instruction, or students who struggle socially or with low motivation. The IWB can be a powerful tool to reach all of our students as individuals and to help them overcome obstacles.

English Language Learners

In our increasingly culturally diverse society, teachers will find linguistic diversity in every classroom. Whether it is the students who speak a dialect or language other than standard English or their parents, language and culture make learners unique and also give each student a different lens for learning. When they feel good about who they are, and when their cultures and identities are valued, students are more open to learning.

Modeling

Modeling is a key strategy for supporting English Language Learners (ELL). Modeling involves demonstrating proper use of the language. Structure and use simple questions related to the meaning of the utterance; this is helpful in shaping a new language. To have a stronger impact, model pronunciation, emphasis, and fluency, and limit cultural idioms.

   English language learners are learning from their peers and are also influenced by digital models, or what they are learning on the Internet. To maximize English Language Learners' development, you can use IWB as a model:

- Use interactive media that use flash. The flash will incorporate sound and visuals to help language learners both hear and see a new concept.
- Link students to games or websites that help translate their native language into English, or that allow them to practice skills in their native languages.

- Use Web 2.0 tools that "read." There are tools that can read aloud what students type or will read an already-formed piece.
- Tell it Twice: This strategy involves having students learn and represent a story twice. Using art media, students can create the scenes in a story to practice the skill of retelling. They can practice telling the story, using a video camera to show the art and the microphone to record the retelling. Finally, the story can be retold a second time in the child's first language. All these retellings can be saved as files and shown to the class, saved for assessment, shared during a parent–teacher conference, or posted publicly, such as on a class blog.

Many resources have been created and many more are posted each day that can model English for students learning to speak a new language. By performing a simple search of *ELL* and *interactive whiteboards*, you can find current and interesting ideas to help support your students.

Valuing Home Language and Culture

The presence of a student's language and culture helps that student build a positive identity and feel included in the classroom. Cummins (1984) holds that home language should be both valued and accepted as an integral part of second-language acquisition and learning. Be sure to remember that bilingualism is valuable for students and has positive social and cognitive benefits for learning. Bringing students' languages and lives into the classroom is even more possible in our digital era. Our world has become smaller, as we can instantly connect with friends and family around the globe. Using the IWB, you can

See Chapter 3 for more on virtual field trips.

- Instantly phone online using Web 2.0 tools. You can use a videocam to communicate with a student's family members overseas to learn about their culture, language, or recent news.
- Encourage your class to participate in a virtual field trip to a place represented by students in the class. ELL students can teach their peers common phrases, their translations into English, and why they are important in their culture.
- Post a world language map and highlight where students' native languages are spoken. Use this same map to show where other languages are spoken. Critically consider why certain languages are spoken in certain countries.
- Connect your students with other students that are experiencing the same transition. Your students can post a blog or Tweet about their experiences, what they have learned, what is challenging, and what they would like to "talk" about.

Dual Language Instruction

Whenever possible, young learners should have the opportunity for dual language instruction, as they build their English language skills on the foundation of their first language. With accessibility to the Internet, you are only a click away from information and resources that can assist your students. You can find websites that translate or read their languages. Your students can refer to some of their favorite websites in their traditional languages and you can use Web 2.0 tools to translate these websites into English. By using the right tools, you can help your students gain access to their languages and help them feel comfortable; at the same time, you learn more about your students' interests and what motivates them.

Traditional

Usually, there is one dominant language of instruction in a classroom. In some classes, bilingual instruction occurs, but normally interactions are limited to the one dominant language. When students who do not speak that language arrive in the class, they struggle to understand what is happening around them. The teacher struggles to assess what these students are able to understand and how to help them bridge the language gap. Teachers are also limited by the selection and availability of first-language resources and by the fact that the school budget cannot keep up with the variety of languages that exist.

IWB Advantage

By using simple translation tools and accessing multilingual websites, students can easily hear text read in their first language and get text translated. Where there once was a language barrier, the doors have been opened wide, as you can search and find materials and translators for many languages. Students come to school with many first languages; these languages are important anchors for learning and can be valued in the classroom using the IWB. You can find websites that translate or interact with your students directly. Students can share their understanding of topics with graphics and speak in their own dialect. They can translate key words and begin to experiment with the learning of the new language. At the same time, other students in the class are enriched by their exposure to another language.

An Interactive Idea for English Language Learning

Objective
To make learning more accessible for English Language Learners.

Hook
Show a relevant video clip to the class that connects with the unit of study on the IWB.

Lesson
1. Translate the video clip using a Web 2.0 tool (e.g., Dot Sub). This will require you to prepare by uploading the video, choosing the language you would like it translated into, and saving the link.
2. Share the translated video with the class. Open a dialogue about words that are similar and words that are very different. For easy reference, tile your screen so that the English video is on one side and the translation is on the other. Have students interact by using the IWB pens to draw lines between words that are the same in different languages.
3. Find an interesting moment and review both videos at the same spot. Let students critically compare the language differences and similarities.
4. Take screenshots and post them on a new document with the words in both languages. For an activity, have ELL students work through the video, matching the vocabulary by dragging and matching the words on the appropriate spot.

Closure
This lesson could spark another that involves students creating their own translated videos, demonstrating the differences in language and culture, including gestures, intonation, volume, and word choice.

Students Who Experience Difficulties

If we know our students well, then the chances that we can find a way to make learning easier and more engaging increases. Teachers are always concerned about how to meet the needs of any student in their class, and especially one who may have a severe challenge. This can be a learning disability, a physical disability, difficulty with memory, or social skills deficits. The IWB provides new possibilities for students with learning challenges, too.

Supporting Students with Learning Challenges

Learning disabilities can be defined as problems with the acquisition, use, and processing of language; they might show up as difficulties with reading, writing, spelling, reasoning, or math. In the elementary years, there are certain practices that support students with learning challenges, and the IWB provides authentic resources that support these practices:

- Keep verbal instructions short; provide repetition of instructions. Using the Record feature of the IWB when guiding through a new task allows your students to go back and hit Play to review instructions as many times as needed prior to beginning.
- Give multiple examples of the same content or skill to clarify meaning. By altering the screen display, you can showcase one or more pages. Displaying a tile effect of pages visually links the information and helps students make connections.
- Allow multiple ways to practice. With the IWB, you can model, engage students in games, and encourage students to use it as a canvas to create.
- Teach students self-monitoring strategies (e.g., Did I understand? What do I have to do now?). With a rubric or checklist, students can easily pull up the file that outlines the success criteria for a given assignment. Students can write short reflections based on those criteria and e-mail their reflections to you for periodic feedback.
- Connect new material to prior knowledge. This can be achieved by brainstorming what you know on a blank screen prior to beginning a task. As the students learn new concepts, they add them to their prior knowledge. By continually adding to the same document, students can remember their original ideas and see the new learning and how it connects.

Supporting Students with Memory Difficulties

When students are attentive and active in learning, retention rates increase dramatically. A study by Eldon Ekwall and William Glasser showed average retention rates related to student engagement:

Lecture	5%
Read material	10%
Audio-visual material	20%
Demonstration	30%
Discussion in groups	50%

Discussion with others	70%
Acquiring by doing	75%
Personal experience	80%
Explain to others and use right away	90%

We can support our students, using the IWB, by

- Gaining and maintaining students' attention by mixing visual and auditory signals, and by giving short, clear directions. Display visual clues using graphics or sound cues on the IWB. Post a "to do" checklist that can be referred to and checked off with a student-selected graphic.
- Using the IWB to incorporate variety, curiosity, and surprise; using interesting lesson hooks and incorporating movements, gestures, voice inflections, visuals, and interesting questions.
- Connecting new vocabulary or knowledge to something meaningful for the student using a familiar graphic or map of the area to prompt the learning.
- Integrating visual and verbal sources. Make sure that the information is available simultaneously and in small chunks, as this helps with encoding information into memory.
- Assessing students on small chunks of information and gradually building up to larger amounts of information, incorporating the smaller chunks as you move ahead. This can be achieved by giving students a chance to practice by creating feedback games and activities that increase in difficulty and repeat prior information.
- Using mnemonic devices. Students can create digital posters for the mnemonic devices using graphic images, and then save them on the desktop for easy reference. Creating a link on the desktop to familiar mnemonics helps students, as they can easily access the information they need.

Supporting Students with Social Skills Deficits

Age-appropriate social interaction is very important for students. Most often, students who have not developed appropriate social skills either have not been exposed to appropriate social skills at home or in another environment, or have difficulty learning social skills through incidental experiences and simple exposure to social situations. Some high-impact strategies for teaching social skills supported by the IWB are

For more information on social stories, see www.thegraycenter.org

- Social scripts or social stories: These are written to target various social situations and teach students what to say and do in them. They provide appropriate language and break down social situations into steps. Social scripts can include emoticons and texting language to make them more meaningful for teenagers.
- Recognizing emotions and facial expressions: Visuals can be accompanied by questions that support social skills development (e.g., Why is this boy happy? What makes him frustrated?)
- Use of media to develop social awareness: TV shows or movies that illustrate various social situations can be paused at various points and questions can be asked (e.g., What is the character feeling? What do you think she will do

now? How will he feel after that?). The video can be played numerous times to expose students to various social situations and then to consolidate understandings around emotions/feelings and actions.

- Teaching social skills in a digital wall: Use a fake social network (see page 102) to model and experiment with what is socially appropriate and how comments affect others.

Traditional

We use a variety of strategies to help reach students who struggle with social interactions. We strive to show them various examples of how to act, what is acceptable or inappropriate, how to judge what to do. We use role-play, puppets, journals, and picture cards. We try our best to catch them in both positive and negative situations and to teach to social action authentically.

IWB Advantage

Using the IWB, you can expand your list of resources. To provide students with more exposure and opportunity to learn, share videos and graphics. Use traditional methods and interact with them in a new way. Students can drag and drop facial expressions to match them with the appropriate term and a possible reaction. They can sort emotions from positive to negative and then drag and match consequences. Interact with movies, by pausing, taking screenshots of the climax, and offering many solutions to the problem. Take all of strategies you are already using and engage your students with a new element—one in which they are standing, sharing their ideas, and presenting while interacting on the IWB. They are taking a risk, critically thinking, and responding to needed information while engaged on the IWB.

For younger students, TV shows about characters from picture books (e.g., Clifford or Franklin) often are about social actions; for older students, using a section of a popular TV show would catch their interest.

An Interactive Idea for Social Skills

Objective
To critically analyze the social dynamic in a video clip.

Hook
Show the selected clip on the IWB.

Lesson
1. Open a discussion: what did students think of the behavior of the characters?
2. Have the students go back to the clip and pause on the moment that demonstrates the strongest emotion. Why did they select that piece? Why is it the strongest emotion? How does the character portray the emotion (using face and body)? Have students use the IWB pens, zoom tools, and highlighters to justify their answers.
3. Take a screenshot of the chosen moment to use for later activities and reflections.
4. Ask students to role play an alternative ending to the scene that would resolve any negative emotions.
5. Discuss the possibilities if negative emotions are not resolved.

> *Closure*
>
> Follow up by saving a copy of the clip on VoiceThreads©. If you create a free account, the class can access the video, pause where they want, and make comments on specific spots. They can use pens to highlight facial expressions or details, just as they do on the IWB. VoiceThreads can be accessed at home and linked to your class blog/website.

Motivating Students

Motivation is an internal state that directs and maintains behavior—teachers can "see" motivation through engagement. A boy who always raises his hand or a girl who works diligently at an assigned task both appear to be motivated. However, there are many students who are slow to start classroom tasks, seem uninterested in class lessons, avoid activities, or even socialize at learning times. There are many reasons why students may or may not be engaged in learning, from home troubles or hunger to lack of interest. Current theories on motivation advocate for both internal and external causes for students' motivation levels. The IWB guides teachers to create a positive environment for learning;

- Empowering students with choice helps to motivate reluctant learners. Using literacy centres (see Chapter 2) allows choice of activities during the literacy block.
- When students receive praise for their efforts on tasks, they are more likely to be motivated than students who are praised for their ability.
- Feedback plays an important role in motivation. When you set up activities on the IWB that provide students with feedback, it supports motivation.
- Rewards and incentives are motivating in the classroom.
- When work is at an appropriate learning level for a student, the student feels competent and, therefore, more motivated to attempt the work.
- Setting goals, either for learning or for performance, support motivation.

See Managing Behavior in Chapter 2 for positive and rewarding ways to motivate students.

Challenging High-Ability Learners

The goal of education is heavily debated among many. However, few disagree that we want students to take learning into their own hands. We want to inspire them to be lifelong learners, to be passionate about learning, and to use everything they have learned to wonder more, ask more, and continually think and learn. The IWB is a tool that can challenge, engage, and empower our students even further.

All students have areas of strength and interest, and areas where they can develop further. As you watch your students grow and develop, you see them excel in certain areas and you celebrate. You praise your students for their eagerness, or reward them for connecting their knowledge or asking more questions. For students who are inspired and ready to extend and challenge their knowledge, the IWB presents a new dynamic for your teaching. When your students have reached this level of engagement, you can also encourage

- Creativity
- Higher-level thinking
- Inquiry-based learning and teaching
- Curriculum compacting

- Flexible groupings
- Extensions using instructional technology
- Use of primary sources in history
- Language arts integration across subject areas

Traditional

Once a student has grasped the taught concepts, they are given extra sheets or more work. They are left to work independently as teachers work to help struggling students master knowledge and skills. We try to match our students' abilities so that they are supporting one another. High-ability learners might be asked to work on the computer independently, accessing various websites or doing further research. When a concept has been grasped, often that is the end of the road and the student needs to wait or assist others until his or her peers catch up.

IWB Advantage

Using the IWB, high-ability learners can be grouped to work collaboratively. They can receive crucial instant feedback from the IWB and peers as they work through relevant games, either teacher-created or accessed through IWB galleries or libraries. They can review concepts taught or add new ideas. They can think ahead to what might be next and plan how to interact with the new information.

An Interactive Idea for Mathematics

Objective
Accelerating students by revealing the 3s pattern in the hundreds chart, identifying the rhythm, and then connecting it with multiplication patterning

Hook
Post an interactive hundreds chart from the IWB software. Engage students by encouraging them to play with the tool and look for patterns.

Lesson
1. Have students identify all the multiples of 3 under 198 and identify the rule. Once students have found the multiples, have them check on the interactive hundreds chart by clicking on the 3s pattern.
2. Further complicate the problem by asking: *What are the similiarities between the multiples? What rules can you create that would work for each multiple of 3?* Students can make a list of rules that works for all of the examples. They can click on numbers that fit the rules and use the pens to identify numbers that need a different rule.
3. Have students justify their answer and use testers above 200 to see if they both fit the rule and are multiples of 3. Have students use the calculator in the IWB toolkit to type in large numbers that meet the rules they have made and see if they are divisible by 3.

Closure
Discuss with the students how a multiple of 3 would be important in our lives. Why would we want to divide 21 by 3? What number stories can they create for larger numbers?

Using the IWB as a tool, we can support our strategies and further challenge students that need an academic challenge by

- Posting websites with games or questions that get progressively more challenging. Using the large screen, students can collaborate, problem solve, and get feedback as they work through the levels
- Posing a problem (e.g., What are differences between the world now and the world during medieval times?) and having students map out what steps they will take, what resources they will use, and what tools they will need to work through and respond to the problem. To find the information, they will want access to books and online resources. They will probably use a large digital map on which they can brainstorm and mark up without the concern of making a permanent mark.
- Posting a topic and having students generate the questions and guide the study. Have them document their resources and ensure they are using a variety of tools and strategies.
- Providing access to a new Web 2.0 tool and having students explore and review it. What would it be useful for? What are the limitations? What advantages does it have over other similar tools?

This screenshot shows how teacher Sarah Barclay supported her students in using Timeline 3D to create a digital timeline of Canadian history from the Quebec Act to the War of 1812. They incorporated visuals and text, with an emphasis on summarizing information. This task was their study tool for their end-of-year assessment. They could easily convert it into a slide show or keep it as a document of information.

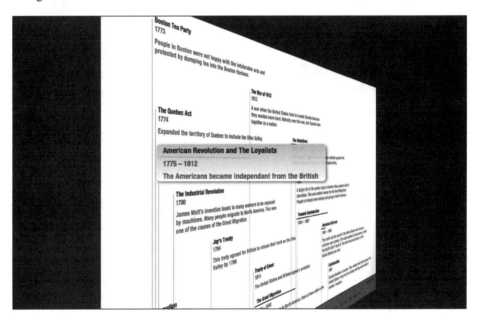

Acknowledgments

To David Booth, who opened the doors for digital literacy and expanded our learning by believing in us and pushing us to question and critically think about our students' learning.

To Shelley Stagg Peterson, who brought us together and encouraged us to think deeply about literacy and learning, inspiring us both to be better educators.

To Mary Macchiusi and Kat Mototsune, for their collaboration and trust in us and for giving us the opportunity to share our experiences and our love of literacy education with others. To Lisa Donohue, for reading and commenting on the manuscript in development.

To all our contributors for sharing their expertise with us: Thomas Babits, Sarah Barclay (our tech support), Lisa Chesworth, Carly Crippin, Meg Davis, Guillaume Dupre, Paul Faggion, Adrienne Fisher, Lisa Fleming, Christie Gordon, Lara Jensen, Mary Kelly, Pam Love, Kathryn O'Brien, Connie vanRijn, Steve Carr, Tom Sharpe, and, most importantly, all our students for teaching and inspiring us.

Thanks to the following for permission to reprint the following images: pages 14, 25, 30, 31, 35, 37–39, 44, 46, 49, 76 (top), 84, 96, 97, 98, 99, 104 (top) SMART Technologies; page 19, Kidblog.org; page 26, Image taken from *Jeu de'association – Je fais de rimes* produced by The Learning Journey International, LLC. © All rights reserved; page 31, Mark Owen; page 45, ©2011 Inspiration® Software, Inc. Diagram created in InspireData® by Inspiration® Software, Inc. Used with permission; page 51, SCRABBLE, the distinctive game board and letter tiles, and all associated logos are trademarks of Hasbro in the United States and Canada and are used with permission. © 2011 Hasbro. All Rights Reserved; page 60, plasq/ Comic Life; page 63, © 2004 LeapFrog Enterprises, Inc.; page 69, Luke & Freebody; page 70, Kent State University, School of Library and Information Science/ KidsClick; page 80, From *Reality Checks* by Tony Stead, copyright © 2006, reproduced with permission of Stenhouse Publishers. www.stenhouse.com; page 90, Jonathan Feinberg/wordle.net; page 91, André Massow; page 101, TC2/File-Maker Inc.; pages 103, 104, ©2011 Inspiration® Software, Inc. Diagram created in Inspiration® by Inspiration® Software, Inc. Used with permission; page 119, BEEDOCS/Timeline 3D.

Professional Resources

Barell, J. (2002) *Developing More Curious Minds.* Alexandria, VA: Association for Supervision and Curriculum Development.

Beers, K. (2003) *When Kids Can't Read: What teachers can do.* Portsmouth, NH: Heinemann.

Bennett, B. & Rolheiser, C. (2001) *Beyond Monet: The artful science of instructional integration.* Toronto, ON: Bookation/Barrie Bennett.

Booth, D. (2008) *It's Critical: Classroom strategies for promoting critical and creative comprehension.* Markham, ON: Pembroke Publishers.

Boushey, G. & Moser, J. (2009) *The CAFE Book: Engaging all students in daily literacy assessment & instruction.* Portland, ME: Stenhouse.

Castek, J., Bevans-Mangelson, J. & Goldstone, B. (2006) "Reading Adventures Online: Five ways to introduce the new literacies of the Internet through children's literature" *The Reading Teacher* 59 (7), 714–28.

Clarke, S. (2008) *Active Learning through Formative Assessment.* London, UK: Hodder Education.

Cummins, J. (1984) *Bilingualism and Special Education.* Clevedon, UK: Multilingual Matters.

Diller, D. (2007) *Making the Most of Small Groups: Differentiation for all.* Portland, ME: Stenhouse

Donohue, L. (2010) *Keepin' It Real: Integrating new literacies with effective classroom practice.* Markham, ON: Pembroke Publishers.

Drake, S.J. & Burns, R. (2004) *Meeting Standards through Integrated Curriculum.* Alexandria, VA: Association for Supervision and Curriculum Development.

Earl, L. (2006) "Assessment—A powerful lever for learning" *Brock Education Journal* 16(1), Brock Education.

Earl, L. (2003) *Assessment as Learning: Using classroom assessment to maximize student learning.* Thousand Oaks, CA: Corwin Press.

Fountas, I.C. & Pinnell, G.S. (2001) *Guiding Readers and Writers, Grades 3–6: Teaching comprehension, genre, and content literacy.* Portsmouth, NH: Heinemann.

Gear, A. (2006) *Reading Power: Teaching students to think while they read.* Markham, ON: Pembroke Publishers.

Gee, J.P. (2003) *What Video Games Have to Teach Us about Learning and Literacy.* New York, NY: Palgrave-Macmillan.

Gray. C. & White, A.L. (2002) *My Social Stories Book.* London, UK: Jessica Kingsley Publishers.

Harvey, S. & Goudvis, A. (2007) *Strategies That Work, 2nd edition: Teaching comprehension for understanding and engagement.* Portland, ME: Stenhouse.

Johnson, D.Q., & Johnson, R.T. (1994) *Learning Together and Alone: Cooperative, competitive, individualistic learning.* Boston MA: Allyn & Bacon.

Lavoie, R., (2007) *The Motivation Breakthrough: Six secrets to turning on the tuned-out child.* New York, NY: Touchstone.

Luke, A. & Freebody, P. (1999) "A Map of Possible Practices: Further notes on the resources model" *Practically Primary* 4(2), 5–9.

Mackey, M. (2002) *Literacies Across Media: Playing the text.* London, UK: Routledge.

McKenzie, J. (2005*) Learning to Question, to Wonder, to Learn.* Bellingham, WA: FNO Press.

Noel, W. & Breau, G. (2005) *Copyright Matters: Some key questions and answers for teachers.* Canada: Council of Ministers of Education.

November, A. (2001) *Empowering Students with Technology.* Thousand Oaks, CA: Corwin Press.

O'Donnell, A.M., D'Amico, M., Schmid, R.F., Reeve, J. & Smith, J.K. (2008) *Educational Psychology: Reflection for action (Canadian Edition).* Mississauga, ON: John Wiley & Sons Canada.

Ontario Ministry of Education (2010) *Growing Success: Assessment, evaluation, and reporting in Ontario schools.*

Ontario Ministry of Education (2007) *Effective Educational Practices for Students with Autism Spectrum Disorders.*

Pink, D. (2005) *A Whole New Mind.* New York, NY: Riverhead Books.

Prensky, M. (2001) "Digital Natives, Digital Immigrants" *On the Horizon* 9(5), MCB University Press.

Pressley, M. (2005) *Reading Instruction that Works: The case for balanced teaching,* 3rd ed. New York, NY: Guildford Press.

Reich, J. & Daccord, T. (2008) *Best Ideas for Teaching with Technology: A practical guide for teachers, by teachers.* Armonk, NY: M.E. Sharpe, Inc.

Robinson, A., Shore, B.M. & Enersen, D. (2007) *Best Practices in Gifted Education: An evidence based guide.* Waco, TX: Prufrock Press.

Routman, R. (2005) *Writing Essentials.* Portsmouth, NH: Heinemann.

Smith, M.W. & Wilhelm, J.D. (2006) *Going with the Flow: How to engage boys (and girls) in their literacy learning.* Portsmouth, NH: Heinemann.

Stagg Peterson, S., Booth, D. & Jupiter, C. (eds) (2009) *Books, Media & the Internet: Children's literature for today's classrooms.* Winnipeg, MB: Portage & Main Press.

Stagg Peterson, S. & Swartz, L. (2008) *Good Books Matter.* Markham, ON: Pembroke Publishers.

Stead, T. (2006) *Reality Checks: Teaching reading comprehension with nonfiction.* Portland, ME: Stenhouse.

Unsworth, L. (2006) *E-literature for Children: Enhancing digital literacy learning.* New York, NY: Routledge Education, Taylor & Francis Group.

Websites

The Critical Thinking Consortium at http://www.tc2.ca/wp/
Educational Technology Quotes at http://www.slideshare.net/tonyvincent/education-technology-quotes
Educational Technology at http://www.edutech.com/default.htm
Simple K12 at http://www.simplek12.com/
Ted: Ideas worth spreading at http://www.ted.com/talks

Index

126